The Baby Book

Sharon Maxwell Magnus
Dr Mark Porter

The pronouns 'he' and 'she' are used
to refer to the baby in alternate chapters.
All chapters do, of course, apply equally
to baby boys and baby girls.

First published in 2000 by
Tesco Stores Limited
Created by Brilliant Books Ltd
84-86 Regent Street
London W1R 5PA

Origination by Colourpath, London
Printed and bound by Butler and Tanner, England

Contents

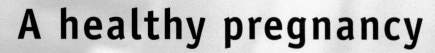

A healthy pregnancy

Your body works hard when
you're pregnant, so this
chapter shows you how to
take special care of yourself
with advice on eating well,
exercise and relaxation

Eating for a healthy baby

Your diet needs to be extra nutritious during pregnancy, but as long as you eat a wide range of foods and follow a few simple guidelines, you and your baby should thrive

WHEN YOU'RE PREGNANT, it's even more important than usual to eat healthily. Your baby depends on your body to provide everything she needs to grow and develop, so a well-nourished mum is more likely to produce a healthy baby. Eating well is important for your own health, too. Your baby is very efficient at taking what she needs from your body, so you need to make sure you have enough essential nutrients for both of you. If you don't, your own health could be affected.

A balanced diet

Eating a variety of foods from each of three important food groups – carbohydrates, fruit and vegetables, and protein – will help ensure that you and your baby get all the nutrients you need. Try to base meals on carbohydrates and fruit or vegetables, and include some protein in each. Steer clear of excessive fat, salt and sugar.

Carbohydrates Eat plenty of these energy-packed foods, which include breakfast cereals (fortified ones and those low in sugar and salt and high in fibre are best), rice, pasta, chapati, potatoes and bread. Choose wholemeal varieties of bread, pasta and breakfast cereals wherever possible.

Fruit and vegetables These provide vital vitamins and minerals, so aim to eat five portions a day. Snacking on fruit and including at least one helping of vegetables with lunch and dinner will help you reach this target. A glass of fruit juice also counts as one portion. Frozen fruit and vegetables

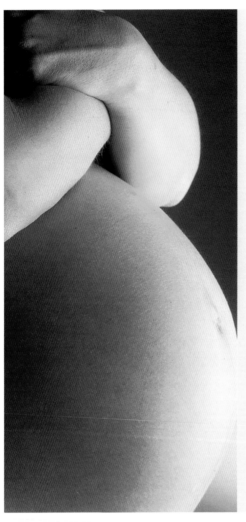

A woman of average weight can expect to gain between 11.5 and 16kg (25-35lbs) during the course of her pregnancy. As a guide, this is made up of: baby, 3.5kg (7½lbs); amniotic fluid, 680g (1½lbs); placenta, 500g (1lb); womb and breasts, 1.5kg (3lbs); extra blood and fluid, 1.5kg (3lbs); fat, 3.5kg (7½lbs). If you are underweight, you will probably gain more and if you are overweight you will probably gain less.

Most women put on about 10 per cent of their total weight gain in the first three months (unless they have severe morning sickness). After that, weight gain is about 500g (1lb) a week, with most weight going on between weeks 24 and 32.

Weight gain usually slows down as you get nearer to the end of your pregnancy.

Pregnancy is not a good time to diet. It's been found that there are more problems associated with not gaining enough weight than there are with gaining too much. On the other hand, there's no need to eat for two. Research has shown a link between excessive weight gain and caesareans, and being overweight also puts a strain on the heart, which is already working much harder than usual.

No extra calories are required for the first six months of pregnancy and only 200 extra a day are needed for the last three – that's the equivalent of just one piece of toast and a banana a day.

can be just as nutritious as fresh and are often more convenient. Canned fruit and vegetables do lose some vitamins and minerals during processing. Buying fruit in natural fruit juice minimises these losses. If you buy canned vegetables, choose those in water with no added salt or sugar.

Protein You need a little more protein when you're pregnant, so try to eat two helpings of protein-rich food every day. This includes meat, fish, eggs, cheese, beans and lentils. If you're vegetarian or vegan, you'll need to combine certain foods to get enough complete protein (see box, page 12).

Special requirements

Folic acid Folic acid is crucial for the healthy development of your baby's nervous system. Taking a daily supplement of folic acid reduces the chances of your baby being affected by spina bifida. For this reason, you should take 400mcg per day as soon as you start trying to conceive until the 12th week of pregnancy. You can buy folic acid supplements from pharmacies or get them on prescription from your doctor. (If you haven't been taking folic acid, start as soon as you think you may be pregnant.)

Vitamin supplements You should be cautious about taking supplements (other than a folic acid supplement) during pregnancy as large doses of some vitamins could harm you and your baby. Eating a healthy diet is the best way to get the nutrients you need. However, there are some supplements formulated for pregnant women. If you would like to take one, discuss this with your doctor or midwife first.

Calcium Getting enough calcium helps keep your bones healthy and is important for the formation of your baby's bones and teeth, too. Try to eat two or three helpings of calcium-rich food each day. A serving would be a third of a pint of milk, a yogurt, or 40g (1½oz) of Cheddar

Canned sardines are a good source of calcium

or other hard cheese (reduced-fat varieties of dairy products provide the same amount of calcium as full-fat varieties). Other sources include tofu, canned sardines and salmon. Vitamin D helps in the absorption of calcium: the best source is sunlight, but it's also found in oily fish and margarine.

Iron When you're pregnant, you'll need extra iron for both yourself and your baby. Red meat, haricot beans, fortified breakfast cereals, canned sardines, egg yolks, dried figs, raisins, prunes and apricots are all good sources (meat and eggs should always be well cooked). Iron is quite difficult for the body to absorb; to aid absorption, try to eat iron-rich food with foods that are rich in vitamin C, such as kiwis, oranges, strawberries, peppers and broccoli. You could try having a glass of orange juice with a bowl of fortified breakfast cereal in the morning, for example. Try to avoid drinking tea or coffee within half an hour of eating an iron-rich meal as they reduce the amount of iron absorbed.

If you are vegetarian, a diet that includes eggs and dairy produce is perfectly adequate for both you and your baby during pregnancy. Make sure you get plenty of iron by eating dark leafy vegetables, beans, dried fruit, fortified cereals and some soya milks. Combine iron-rich foods with a vitamin C-rich food to ensure better absorption.

If you are vegan (eating no animal produce at all) up your protein intake with plenty of rice, pasta, bread, soya, tofu, lentils, beans and nuts (avoid peanuts, though, if you have a family history of allergy). Whereas animal proteins contain all the amino acids necessary for health, vegetable proteins contain only some, so they should be combined with wheat/grain products to make them a complete protein. Beans on toast, dhal with chapati, lentil soup with bread, bean and pasta salad and vegetarian lasagne are examples of well-balanced vegan meals.

If you don't eat dairy produce, you also need to be sure of getting enough calcium. Some brands of soya milk are fortified with it, and tofu, broccoli, tahini, nan bread, spinach and dried figs are all good sources.

Vitamin B12 is not found in any plant foods so it's wise to eat one serving each day of a food that is fortified with it, such as breakfast cereals, certain yeast extracts, soya milk and soya mince. It's a good idea to see your GP if you think you need a supplement.

Foods to take care with

There are some foods that you should avoid during pregnancy because of the effect they could have on both you and your baby. You should also take special care when you're preparing certain foods.

Listeria   To protect your baby from listeria monocytogenes, a bacteria that can cause miscarriage or premature birth, avoid the following foods:

● Soft, ripened cheeses, such as Brie and Camembert

● Blue-veined cheeses, such as Danish Blue, Stilton and Roquefort

● All unpasteurised milk and anything made from it

● Pâté of all kinds.

You should also take care with cook-chill meals. These must be reheated until they are piping hot right through and then served immediately. Ready-made frozen meals are safer but they should also be served piping hot all the way through.

Toxoplasmosis is a microscopic parasite that can cause defects such as blindness or brain damage. To protect your baby, take the following precautions with food:

Blue-veined cheeses and soft-boiled or raw eggs should be avoided in pregnancy

● Avoid all unpasteurised milk and any products made from it.

● Avoid all raw or under-cooked meats, such as Parma ham.

● Cook all meat thoroughly.

● Wash your hands immediately after handling raw meat.

Toxoplasmosis can also be contracted via contact with animals (see page 15) and may be present in soil, so:

● Wash all fruit and vegetables before eating, even those that are pre-packed and ready washed.

● Wear gloves when gardening and wash your hands afterwards.

Salmonella This causes food poisoning, which can really lay a pregnant woman low. Steer clear of salmonella by avoiding these foods:

Retinol If vitamin A from animal sources (retinol) is eaten in large quantities, there may be an increased risk of birth defects. For this reason, you should avoid liver and liver products, such as pâté and cod liver oil, and any supplements containing vitamin A.

Peanuts Eating peanuts during pregnancy may increase the chances of your child developing a potentially serious allergy to peanuts. If you have any allergies, such as asthma, eczema, hayfever or a nut allergy, or if anyone in your family has an allergy, avoid peanuts and foods containing peanut products such as peanut butter and unrefined groundnut oil. Even if you have no allergies, it's not a good idea to eat large quantities of peanuts while pregnant.

Wash all fruit and vegetables thoroughly before eating them, even those that are pre-packed and ready washed

● Raw or soft-boiled eggs, and any food that may contain them, such as home-made mayonnaise and home-made ice cream (Shop-bought varieties are fine.)

● Under-cooked chicken and turkey

● Shellfish and smoked or cured meat and fish, unless bought from a reputable store, pre-packed and date stamped

● Soft-whip ice cream (the sort sold by ice-cream vans).

Coffee, tea, cola and cocoa These all contain caffeine, a mild stimulant. Although the jury is still out on whether drinking large amounts of caffeine causes problems for babies, current government guidelines say that pregnant women should drink no more than five caffeine-containing drinks a day. Try decaffeinated teas and coffees, or fruit teas, instead. Fruit juice makes a healthy alternative to cola.

Protecting your baby

To create the very best conditions for the baby growing inside you, you need to take extra care with alcohol and medicine while you're pregnant, and to cut out smoking completely

PREGNANCY IS THE PERFECT TIME to start taking more care of yourself and to replace bad habits with good ones, for your baby's sake as well as your own.

Smoking

Smoking during pregnancy harms your baby. Babies of smokers are more likely to be small and to be born prematurely. Smokers are at more risk of miscarrying and having placental problems, and may suffer more severely from morning sickness. Research indicates smoking may affect the development of the baby's brain.

Children who live with smokers are more likely to suffer a cot death than those living with non-smokers. They're also more prone to asthma, chest infections and childhood cancers. It's best to stop smoking altogether, preferably before you get pregnant.

How to **stop smoking**

- **Choose the day** when you're going to give up. Shortly before the day, throw away all your cigarettes, matches and lighters, and remove ashtrays from your home.
- **Avoid** situations where you'll be tempted to smoke. If you only smoke in the pub, go somewhere else instead. If you normally buy cigarettes from a certain shop, take a different route.
- **Drink** plenty of water or fruit juice. Keep a glass handy. Instead of having a cigarette, take a walk, phone a friend, clean the windows or go for a swim.
- **Be prepared** for withdrawal symptoms, such as a sore throat or feeling grumpy. These are normal and will disappear.
- **Ask your friends** for support. The charity Quit has a helpline, called Quitline, staffed by professional counsellors who can also help (see page 169).
- **Enlist** your partner's support. If he's a smoker, encourage him to give up at the same time (his smoking will also affect your baby). If he won't give up, ask him not to leave cigarettes lying around and to smoke outside the house.
- **Reward yourself** for giving up – you'll probably have saved a lot of money.
- **Nicotine patches** etc are not advisable in pregnancy. Don't use them without medical supervision.

Instead of alcohol, have a glass of fruit juice

approach, then, is either to give up alcohol altogether or just to have the occasional glass – you may find that you go off alcohol anyway. The Royal College of Obstetricians and Gynaecologists suggests that pregnant women should drink no more than one unit a day.

If you had one evening of heavy drinking before you knew you were pregnant, don't worry. Evidence shows it's regular heavy drinking that causes problems.

Medication

If you have to take regular medication, let your doctor know before you become pregnant. That way, if your medicine could affect your baby, you may be prescribed a safer alternative or have your dosage altered.

Before you take any drugs – even over-the-counter ones – in pregnancy, or when you are trying to conceive, talk to your pharmacist or doctor first and check they're suitable for pregnant women. It's best to avoid all medication if you can, but this isn't always possible.

Alcohol

Drinking too much alcohol in pregnancy is bad for your baby – any more than 15 units of alcohol a week poses a serious risk (a unit is a glass of wine, a measure of spirits or half a pint of lager or beer). The most serious form of damage is fetal alcohol syndrome, which causes severe learning difficulties in the baby. The best

Animals

Cats can carry toxoplasmosis (see page 12) in their faeces so avoid clearing out litter trays while pregnant. If you have to do it yourself, wear gloves and wash your hands thoroughly afterwards. If you live on a farm or are involved with animals, avoid contact with goats, sheep and cows, as they can carry illnesses harmful to unborn babies. You also shouldn't help with lambing. If you think you may be at high risk of toxoplasmosis, tell your doctor or midwife, who may offer you a test for reassurance.

Exercise and relaxation

Pregnancy, labour and giving birth make great demands on your body, so it's important to keep in good shape, whether you continue with your normal exercise or try a new one

THERE ARE LOTS OF GOOD REASONS for keeping fit while you're pregnant. Exercise not only helps to ease many of the common aches and pains of pregnancy, it produces feel-good chemicals that give you a natural high and also helps prepare your body for the hard work of giving birth (although it doesn't necessarily make labour easier). It will also help you recover more quickly after the birth.

Adapting your usual routine

Being pregnant puts additional strain on your body so, even if you exercise regularly, it's best to do only two thirds of your normal routine and to ease up even more during the last three months of pregnancy.

Your normal exercise or dance class should be fine, provided the teacher knows that you're pregnant and is trained to modify your exercises accordingly, and provided you pace yourself rather than going flat out. Your softened ligaments make your joints more vulnerable during pregnancy, so warming up is even more important than usual. For the same reason, you should choose low-impact, rather than high-impact, work to avoid any damage.

Take similar precautions at the gym: tell the instructor you're pregnant, avoid high-impact work and don't overdo it. When you're pregnant it's easier to hurt your back, so avoid lifting heavy weights.

What type of exercise?

If you didn't have a regular fitness routine before you became pregnant, try some of these safe and gentle exercises:

- Swimming builds strength, suppleness and stamina and, because the water supports your weight, is perfect for pregnancy.
- Brisk walking costs nothing, is safe and gentle, and builds stamina and fitness.
- Antenatal exercise classes and yoga and aquanatal classes for pregnant women can help you get fitter and feel relaxed. Ask your midwife what's available locally.

During pregnancy, you should avoid any exercise that involves the risk of falling, including sports such as horse-riding, skiing and water skiing.

Strengthen your pelvic floor

Pelvic floor exercises are the single most important type of exercise you can do during pregnancy. Your pelvic floor is made up of a set of muscles which support the womb, the bladder and the lower bowel. Pregnancy and labour put a great strain on these muscles. Keeping them well toned can help you avoid stress incontinence – leaking when you run, cough or sneeze – which many women experience after giving birth.

One way to work out where your pelvic floor muscles are is to stop your urine midstream – the muscles you use to do this are your pelvic floor muscles. Contracting the muscles to stop the flow is the same as the action you use to exercise the muscles. (Don't stop your urine repeatedly – it could cause an infection.)

Once you've identified your pelvic floor muscles, you should aim to do five sets of five contractions every day. There are two ways to do this. Whichever method you choose, concentrate on working the pelvic floor muscles alone – try not to clench your buttock or stomach muscles too.

The slow squeeze Draw the muscles up slowly as if they were a lift, stopping at various levels. Hold the muscles as tight as you can ('at the top floor'), then gradually release them as if the lift were returning 'to the bottom floor'. Relax and repeat. Once you can do this, try stopping 'at the first floor' on the way up and down.

The sudden clench Clench your back passage as if you're trying to stop a bowel movement, draw in your vagina as if you were gripping a tampon and pretend you are trying to stop passing urine, all at the same time. Hold the muscles tight for five seconds. Relax and repeat.

The beauty of these exercises is that you can do them anywhere – while you're washing up, queuing at the checkout, even sitting at your desk. Ask your antenatal teacher for help if you're having difficulties understanding what to do.

Look after your back

Back pain is very common in pregnant women. A number of factors work together to cause this: the ligaments that hold the joints together soften in pregnancy, your changing shape means your body is not aligned as it normally is, and your body is carrying

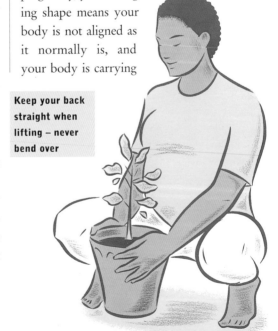

Keep your back straight when lifting – never bend over

Pelvic tilts

Pelvic tilts can help relieve back pain and strengthen the abdominal muscles, and can also ease pain in the early stages of labour. Tilting your pelvis takes the weight off the uterus onto your buttocks and abdomen.

Get down onto all fours on the floor and make sure your back is flat, like a table. Squeeze your tummy and buttock muscles tight and tilt your pelvis forward, so your back starts to look like a humpback bridge.

Hold for a count of five and release. Repeat several times. Breathe out as you tighten the muscles and in as you relax. The more you do this exercise, the easier it will become. You can also do it standing and lying down.

the weight of your growing baby. Backache during pregnancy may not be completely preventable, but you can minimise it by following these simple rules:

Stand right Stand tall, tuck in your buttocks and tighten your stomach muscles. If you have bad posture or your back isn't flexible, try to improve your suppleness. Sit cross-legged against a wall, lengthen your spine and press your back into the wall. This should help you feel the correct way to hold yourself.

Sit right When you're sitting at a desk, make sure that your feet are flat on the floor and that your bottom is well back and supported by the back of the chair. When you

sit up from a lying down position, roll onto your side and use your arms to push yourself up sideways.

Lift right Try to avoid heavy lifting if at all possible. Ask for help with loading your shopping into the car at the checkout and get someone else to unload at the other end.

If you have to lift, keep your back straight and bend your knees until you are at the same level as the object you want to lift. Stand close to whatever you're lifting and keep it next to your body as you pick it up. Keep your back straight while you lift, using your legs to do the work. Alternatively, lower yourself onto one knee. If you need to work at floor level, kneel on the floor rather than bending down.

Relaxation in pregnancy

Relaxation is important in anyone's life, but during pregnancy, when you're combining work with thinking about the future, or are already a mother, finding a quiet time for yourself can be hard. However, making time to relax will help make your pregnancy less stressful. Relaxation can also help in labour, as calming techniques can ease labour pains, particularly in the early stages.

A quick and easy relaxation exercise is to lie down, close your eyes and, starting with your toes, tense your muscles in turn and then let go. As you work your way up to your forehead, you'll find your body feels increasingly heavy and relaxed.

Yoga As well as being extremely relaxing, yoga increases flexibility and strength, and improves circulation and breathing. Some positions, such as squatting, can be used in childbirth. Joining a class will give you a quiet, relaxing time to concentrate on yourself and your baby. Not all yoga positions are suitable for pregnancy, so choose a class specially for pregnant women. Details of classes are available from The Active Birth Centre (see page 168).

Massage This is another excellent way of relaxing during pregnancy and can also be used to relieve backache and other muscular aches in labour. There are classes and videos on massage for pregnant women (ask your midwife for details of local classes), but you can also find out what suits you best simply by practising with your partner or birth partner. Ask your partner to massage your shoulders and upper back, using circular movements, or to massage your hips on either side of the base of your spine, again in a circular motion. Always follow these important rules:

● Always massage around the spine, never on the spine itself.

● Use a simple oil, such as baby oil or grapeseed oil. Never use aromatherapy oils unless a reputable practitioner or pharmacist, who knows you are pregnant, has specifically recommended them. Massage with essential oils isn't advised during the first three months of pregnancy.

Sleep well

Getting a good night's sleep is often easier said than done during pregnancy, especially during the final months. As you grow bigger, you may find it increasingly difficult to get comfortable in bed.

• **Experiment** with different positions and use cushions or extra pillows to help support your bump.

• **If worries** about your pregnancy or life with a baby are keeping you awake, try to make a time early in the day to think through whatever is bothering you.

• **Try** having a regular time for going to bed and for getting up.

• **A hot** milky drink or a cup of camomile tea before bedtime will help you relax.

• **Avoid** heavy, rich meals or fatty food in the evening.

• **Soak** in a hot bath before going to bed to relax your muscles.

Imagine a soothing scene – a sunny meadow, perhaps. Now imagine yourself inside that scene...

Visualisation Imagining a peaceful scene can help you relax and may also be used to relieve anxiety during early labour. Most relaxation tapes feature visualisation exercises as well as soothing sounds, such as bird-song or waves, to aid relaxation. Alternatively, try this simple visualisation exercise whenever you need to calm down. Sit or lie down on your side and close your eyes. Breathe in and out slowly, but try not to make your breathing laboured. Concentrate all your attention on your breathing. Once you feel relaxed, imagine a soothing scene – a sunny meadow, perhaps. Now imagine yourself inside that scene, maybe lying in the grass. Feel the sun on your face, hear the birds singing, smell the grass... After a while, let the scene fade away and stay calm and still for a while, enjoying the feeling of peace.

Looking after your body

Don't be surprised if your skin, hair and nails start behaving differently in pregnancy – it's completely normal. All you need to do is make a few minor changes to your beauty routine

PREGNANCY HORMONES can affect your appearance in various ways, but understanding what's going on will make you feel more confident about the way you look.

Your skin

You may find that pregnancy makes your skin look fantastic, with increased circulation giving you a healthy bloom. However, for some women, the opposite happens and they develop spots for the first time, particularly during the first three months of pregnancy. If this happens, apply the minimum of moisturiser and use a concealer.

Pregnancy makes the skin's pigmentation darker and can cause dark patches on your face (chloasma) which may intensify in the sun, so use a high-factor sun-screen. The patches usually fade after the birth.

As your tummy expands, you may find it begins to itch. Use a mild soap and wash with warm, rather than hot, water to prevent oil loss. Afterwards, moisturising will help prevent dryness, although it won't prevent stretch marks; these may look quite prominent during pregnancy, but most fade to a more silvery tone afterwards. In the

later stages, you may also discover a dark line (linea nigra) running down the centre of your stomach. This, too, will fade after the birth. Some women develop thread-like veins on the face – again, these will fade after the birth.

Your hair

You'll probably find that your hair looks thicker during pregnancy. This is because pregnancy hormones slow hair loss, hence the tendency for more of it to fall out once the baby's born. If yours starts to thin or fall out during pregnancy, talk to your midwife in case you have a nutritional deficiency.

Avoid permanent colorants when you're pregnant and use the wash-in-wash-out or semi-permanent kind. Permanent colours contain strong chemicals and, because your hair texture may change during pregnancy, they may not give the effect you want.

Your nails

You may find your nails are more prone to splitting and breaking. If so, wear rubber gloves when you do the washing-up and be liberal with the hand cream.

Common complaints

When your body's doing something as special as growing a baby, there are bound to be some small discomforts. However, most will be minor irritations which can be easily relieved

EVEN IF YOU HAVE a generally healthy pregnancy, as most women do, you'll probably experience one or two common complaints. There are often simple solutions to these problems although, in some cases, you simply have to wait until a particular stage of your pregnancy passes.

Bleeding gums

You'll need to take extra care of your teeth throughout pregnancy as pregnancy hormones soften the gums, which can cause bleeding and make you more susceptible to gum disease. Brushing carefully twice a day and flossing can help prevent problems. Pregnancy is a good time to see your dentist as check-ups are free for NHS patients throughout pregnancy and for a year after the birth. However, if possible, try and steer clear of dental X-rays during pregnancy.

Breathlessness

It's not unusual in the latter half of pregnancy to experience a mild feeling of breathlessness when you walk. This happens because your growing baby prevents your lungs from expanding fully and because of changes to your circulation. It's particularly likely if you are carrying your baby high or in a breech position. Sitting down until the sensation passes may help. However, if breathlessness is severe and you have chest pains or your fingers turn blue, see your doctor. Breathlessness earlier on in pregnancy, especially if it's coupled with extreme tiredness, may be a sign of anaemia (see page 54), so visit your doctor.

Constipation and piles

Many women experience constipation in the middle and later months of pregnancy, together with the bloating and cramps that it causes. To minimise the problem, drink at least six glasses of water a day and gradually increase your intake of fibre-rich food, such as wholemeal bread, bran breakfast cereal, muesli, baked beans and peas.

Constipation makes haemorrhoids (piles) more likely. These are varicose veins around the anus which can become itchy and sore, and may bleed. If you experience rectal bleeding, see your GP, as this can be a symptom of other illnesses. To alleviate the problem, follow the guidelines to prevent

constipation and lie on your side, rather than your back, to sleep. Your pharmacist may also be able to recommend a cream suitable for pregnant women.

Cramp

Cramp in your leg muscles can occur at any time during pregnancy. A third of women get it and it's usually worse in the second half of pregnancy. Although no-one is sure why it occurs, it may be linked to calcium deficiency, so eating calcium-rich foods such as leafy green vegetables, tofu and dairy produce could help. Exercising regularly is good as it improves the circulation, and support stockings (worn in the evening and in bed) can work wonders. Avoid too much

standing and rest your feet on a pillow in bed. If cramp does strike, stretch the muscle by pushing your heel out and pulling your toes towards you. Massage may also help.

Cravings

Cravings for oranges and other fruit, milk and bread are common and even healthy in the first months of pregnancy. However, beware if you crave endless chocolate or other foods that prevent you from eating a varied and nutritious diet. Occasionally, women have cravings for non-foods, such as chalk or charcoal (this is known as pica). If this applies to you, talk it over with your midwife – it's much more common than you might think.

Frequent urination

Needing to go to the loo more often is common in the first three and last three months of pregnancy. This is because your bladder is squeezed by your growing baby and because the pregnancy hormone, progesterone, causes your bladder muscles to relax. Frequent urination should only be a concern if you experience pain or a hot, burning sensation. Either of these could indicate cystitis, a urinary infection that can spread to the kidneys if left untreated.

Indigestion

Indigestion tends to occur in the middle and later months of pregnancy as your baby takes up more space in your abdomen and cramps your digestive organs. Changes in hormone levels also make heartburn, a burning sensation in your chest, more likely. Eating little and often can help. Have a drink half an hour after a meal rather than with your food and avoid spicy foods, alcohol, fizzy drinks, acidic drinks such as orange juice, and fatty foods such as bacon. Leave at least an hour's gap between finishing dinner and going to bed, as lying down can make indigestion worse.

Itching

Many women suffer from itching during pregnancy, especially around the abdomen. Careful skin care can relieve discomfort (see page 22). However, severe generalised itching in late pregnancy may be a symptom of

Ginger can help alleviate morning sickness, so try nibbling on a ginger biscuit when nausea strikes

obstetric cholestasis, a rare liver disorder. A blood test will confirm the diagnosis and your baby may need to be delivered early.

Morning sickness

This is very common, particularly in the first three months, with seven out of ten women experiencing it. A few women suffer throughout their pregnancy. It's thought that morning sickness is caused by fluctuating hormone levels, and stress can make it worse. Despite its name, morning sickness can strike at any time of day.

Women often worry that if sickness is preventing them from eating, their baby will be undernourished. In fact, nature allows your baby first call on any nutrients available. It's the mother who's more likely to end up lacking in nutrients. For around three in 1000 women, morning sickness is so severe that hospital treatment is needed.

Morning sickness can be triggered by fried, fatty, rich or spicy foods, coffee or smells like perfume, cigarette smoke or petrol. Ease feelings of nausea by eating little and often. Keep a pack of plain biscuits by the bed and nibble one before getting up. Base other small frequent meals on carbohydrate foods such as bread, cereals, pasta, potatoes and rice. Drink plenty of fluids to replace those lost through vomiting. Some women find that ginger helps, so try a ginger biscuit or a drink such as ginger ale.

There is some evidence that a deficiency in zinc may make women more susceptible to morning sickness. Good sources of zinc include meat, cheese, wholegrain products, and pumpkin and sesame seeds.

If you feel sick in the evening, tiredness may make it worse, so rest in the day. Some women swear by acupressure bands, usually used for travel sickness. Complementary therapies may help, too (see pages 28-29).

Tiredness

The only way to cope with tiredness in early pregnancy is to rest as much as you can. However, if the tiredness is combined with breathlessness, see your GP, as this may indicate anaemia (see page 54).

During the last three months of pregnancy, tiredness is inevitable. Try and have a couple of weeks off work before your due date so you can start adapting to your new life and rest in preparation for labour.

Varicose veins

Varicose veins may appear in mid and late pregnancy and are more likely if other members of your family have them. They occur when valves in the veins start to fail, which means blood flow becomes less efficient, causing blood to 'pool'. As a result, some veins stand out and often look bruised and purple. They may itch or ache.

You can help prevent varicose veins by avoiding standing or sitting still for long periods, doing plenty of exercise, avoiding constipation and straining, watching your weight gain and wearing support tights. Put these on first thing in the morning, before the veins have a chance to swell. Sitting with your feet up will also help. Avoid sitting cross-legged as this restricts circulation.

Vaginal discharge and thrush

It's quite common to have more discharge than normal during pregnancy, particularly in the later stages. If it's thin, white and doesn't irritate you, it's nothing to worry about. However, if it's thick, smells and you have itching or soreness around the vaginal area, it may be thrush or another infection, so tell your doctor or midwife. Your doctor may prescribe an anti-fungal cream but, in the meantime, bathing in water with a little salt added may help.

Try and have a couple of weeks off before your due date so you can rest in preparation for labour

Complementary therapies

Complementary therapies can help ease some of the common complaints of pregnancy, as well as being beneficial during labour. However, it's important to be aware that just because something is 'natural', it doesn't mean it's safe. If you're interested in using any complementary therapy while pregnant, it's vital to check it's suitable first. Ideally, you should have a consultation with a reputable practitioner.

Acupuncture   Research suggests that both acupuncture and acupressure are particularly effective in treating morning sickness, backache and sciatica, turning breech babies and for pain-relief during labour. Indeed, quite a few hospitals now offer acupuncture. Contact the British Acupuncture Council for details of qualified practitioners (see page 168).

Aromatherapy   This is especially good for backache, tiredness and constipation. Essential oils obtained from herbs, seeds and spices are best avoided whilst those from citrus, woods and flowers are generally useful in pregnancy. Always consult a qualified practioner if there is any doubt.

Chiropractic   Chiropractic involves the manipulation of the muscular and skeletal structure. It's good for backache, cramp and other muscular aches and pains. Always consult a qualified practitioner.

Herbalism   Herbalism can be used to treat a wide range of ailments in pregnancy. For example, an infusion of camomile, lemon balm, peppermint or ginger will help settle the stomach and ease the symptoms of morning sickness. An infusion of nettle leaves taken throughout pregnancy will provide a useful tonic that's rich in iron, and raspberry leaves taken in the third trimester will help prepare the uterus for childbirth and ease labour.

There are a number of herbs that should not be taken in pregnancy because they stimulate the uterus, so always consult a qualified medical herbalist (see page 169).

Homeopathy The aim of homeopathy is to treat the whole person, not just the symptom. The principle behind the remedies is to treat like with like, in minute quantities: for instance, a substance that causes nausea will be used to treat nausea.

Homeopathy can be used to treat a number of pregnancy ailments. The treatment involves administering a tiny amount of active ingredient, measured according to the patient's individual symptoms and constitution. The majority of remedies are derived from plants, some from minerals and some from animal sources, and many are available from your local chemist. One very useful homeopathic remedy is arnica, which is recommended to heal bruising from labour – it can be taken for a week before labour to help prevent bruising.

If you want to use homeopathy during pregnancy and labour, make sure you see a qualified homeopath. Contact the British Homeopathic Association for a list of medically-qualified homeopaths in your area. For homeopathic labour kits, contact The Active Birth Centre and The Pregnancy Shop (see pages 168-169).

Osteopathy This uses manipulation of the bones, joints and muscles to relieve and treat pain, so it can be very good for pregnancy aches and pains such as backache, pain in the legs and bottom (sciatica) and other muscular aches. Osteopaths can also help you to adapt your posture during

pregnancy to help prevent back pain. Osteopathy may also help relieve digestive problems and constipation. Contact the Osteopathic Information Service (see page 169) for more information and details of local practitioners.

The herb valerian is a useful sedative and relaxant and can also help relieve muscle pain

How will you feel?

It's not just your body that changes when you're pregnant – your emotions can become unfamiliar, too. It's reassuring to know that the ups and downs you'll experience are quite normal

FOR MOST WOMEN, pregnancy – especially the first one – is an emotional roller coaster. You may feel thrilled and elated one moment, worried as to how you'll cope or whether your baby will be healthy the next. You may look forward to motherhood or wonder if it will mean loss of freedom. However you feel, you'll have lots of adjustments to make as you come to terms with the fact that you'll soon be a mother.

These kinds of fluctuating emotions are normal. Every life change brings doubts and worries as well as hopes and joys, and pregnancy is no exception. In addition, many women find that changing hormone levels make them weepy and moody, causing them to burst into tears at things which might previously have left them unmoved. Although these mood-swings can be confusing, they are normal and will probably lessen as pregnancy progresses.

Your partner's feelings

Your partner, too, is having to come to terms with his changing role. Although he may be excited at the prospect of becoming a father, he may also be worried about you,

For single parents, pregnancy can be a stressful time as well as an exciting one. You can help yourself by:
• **Getting as much** support as you can, both practical and emotional, from parents, friends and colleagues.
• **Talking to** your midwife about what help is available locally. There may be an organisation for single parents you can join, for example.
• **Attending** a local antenatal class. Not only will it help you prepare for the birth, but you will also meet other women who are about to become mothers.
• **Thinking about** who you want as a birth partner and asking well in advance.
• **Even if** you meet with disapproval from your family or people who don't know you, concentrate on all the good things that you can offer your baby.

Going it alone

or about coping financially, or even feeling left out. Understanding that this is a challenging time for both of you and trying to be supportive towards each other is important, and is good practice for when your baby arrives. Other ways to help yourselves as a couple include:
• Make time for each other and try to do things together. Share your hopes and fears.

Sex in pregnancy

How you feel about sex in pregnancy will depend largely on how your pregnancy goes. Some women find being pregnant makes them feel extra sexy and that sex is even more satisfying. However, intense morning sickness in the first three months and feeling large and ungainly in the last are not good aphrodisiacs. If you're not feeling well, all you may want to do in bed is sleep.

Sex is generally safe during pregnancy and won't harm your baby. However, if you experience vaginal bleeding afterwards, or have had a threatened miscarriage, talk to your doctor. Your growing body may also make some positions more awkward than previously. Woman on top or man behind may be more comfortable.

Sometimes you may find that your sexual feelings are out of step with your partner's. You may feel keen while he is anxious, or exhausted when he is enthusiastic. If this happens, it's important to talk about it and to show physical affection in other ways, such as cuddling, kissing or stroking.

● If you can afford it, this is a great time to have a last holiday as a couple together.
● Most antenatal classes will have at least one session that partners can attend. There are also classes specifically for couples.
● Try to keep up any activities you enjoyed together before pregnancy.

Travel tips

● **The best time** to take a final pre-baby holiday together is after 12 weeks, when morning sickness and the risk of miscarriage subside, but before the last three months of pregnancy when your size − and the possibility of premature delivery − increase.

● **Many airlines** won't carry a pregnant woman after a certain number of weeks (often 28 or 32). Check before you book.
● **Travel health insurance** is vital if you're going abroad just in case you develop pregnancy complications.

● **In countries** outside western Europe, north America and Australia, steer clear of stomach upsets by buying bottled water and avoiding salads and any fruit you haven't peeled yourself. Wherever you go, stick to the usual food safety guide-lines (see pages 12-13).

A working pregnancy

If, like many women these days, you go out to work, there's no reason why you shouldn't be able to carry on with your job for most of your pregnancy as long as you feel fit and well

WOMEN'S EXPERIENCE OF WORK during pregnancy varies enormously. Some sail through, enjoying the support of colleagues and showing off their scan pictures. Others feel tired or have bosses who blanche at the very thought of a baby.

While you're still at work

Whatever your work environment, the law protects you from being sacked because of your pregnancy and from having to work in a way, or with materials, which may endanger your health or your baby's health. For instance, if you normally work with X-rays or certain chemicals, such as lead, or if you perform regular heavy lifting, your employer must, by law, find suitable alternative work or suspend you on full pay if no alternative is available. Many pregnant women worry about working in front of a VDU, but there is no evidence that this poses any threat to you or your baby, although it is always a good idea to get up to stretch your legs every hour.

While being pregnant doesn't mean spending nine months with your feet up, it isn't a good time to push yourself to the

limit either. Take regular breaks and try to spend your lunch hour relaxing and actually eating lunch, rather than rushing round, lugging huge bags of shopping. If getting to work means a strenuous commute in the rush hour, ask your boss if you could start and finish later or even do some work from home. Many are more flexible than you might think. If you're in an active job, such as teaching or nursing, do rest in the evening and take your breaks.

Giving up work

To some extent, when you stop work is up to you. You can work as late into your pregnancy as you like, or stop, at the earliest, 11 weeks before your estimated date of delivery. Generally, most doctors prefer you to stop about a month before your due

Pregnancy isn't a time to push yourself, and if travelling to and from work in the rush hour is proving a real strain, ask your boss if you can change your hours

date so that you can get used to a different pace of life and go into the birth rested rather than exhausted. If you have twins, you'll probably have to stop earlier.

Protecting your rights

You don't have to tell your employer that you're pregnant or planning to go on maternity leave until three weeks before the date that you wish to stop work. However, if you want to take time off for antenatal appointments and to make use of your health and safety rights, you'll need to inform him/her well before this.

When you do inform your employer, let him/her know, in writing, that you're pregnant, your estimated date of delivery (EDD) and when you wish to start maternity leave. You may be asked to produce pregnancy forms, such as the MATB1, which you'll get from your midwife or GP at about 26 weeks of pregnancy. Putting all the details in writing will help protect your maternity rights.

Maternity benefits

The law on maternity leave and maternity pay is extremely complex. If you work in a large company, your personnel officer can explain the provisions that affect you. However, if you work in a small company, you may need additional advice. If you don't understand what your rights are, or have

problems at work which you feel stem from your pregnancy, it's worth contacting your trade union, the Citizens' Advice Bureau, or The Maternity Alliance (see page 169).

The provisions listed in the 'Your rights' panel apply to babies born during 2000, although at the time of writing the government hadn't finalised the starting date. If you have your baby before the new provisions are introduced, you will only be entitled to 14 weeks' maternity leave and to maternity absence after two years' service. As the amounts of Statutory Maternity Pay (SMP) and Maternity Allowance vary from year to year, no amounts are included here.

Your **rights**

- **Every employee**, whether full time or part time, is entitled to 18 weeks' maternity leave. However, you must let your employer know that you intend to take this leave at least three weeks before you want to stop work.
- **You are entitled** to paid time off for antenatal appointments. (But you must let your employer know that you are attending an appointment, rather than simply disappearing from work.)
- **You cannot** be sacked or made redundant because of pregnancy. It makes no difference how long you've worked for your employer or whether you work full or part time.
- **Many women** who are employed are entitled to Statutory Maternity Pay (SMP) for 18 weeks. If you are self-employed, have worked for your employer for only a short time, or earn less than the SMP threshold, you may be entitled to Maternity Allowance or Incapacity Benefit. Contact your local benefits agency for information.
- **If you have worked** for your employer for more than one year and 11 weeks by the time the baby is due, you can take extended maternity absence. This is effectively an extra 15 weeks' unpaid leave, which you can take after your paid maternity leave. If you work for a small company (less than five employees), your employer does not have to give you your job back or provide a reasonable alternative after extended maternity absence if he/she can show that it is not practical to do so.
- **You are entitled** to accrue holiday during maternity leave and, in the main, to keep benefits such as private health insurance and your company car.
- **Parental leave**, to be introduced in 2000, allows you and your partner to take up to three months unpaid leave. At the time of writing, details had not been finalised.

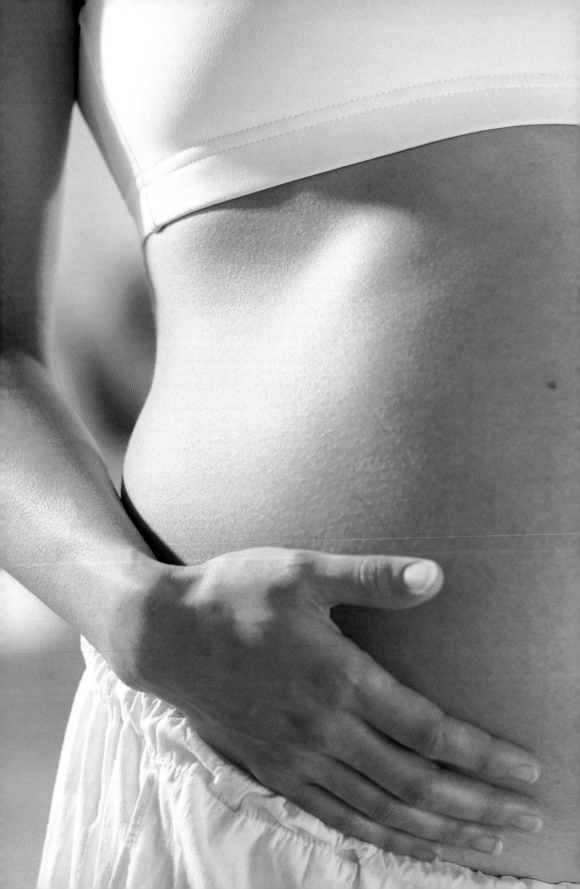

Your antenatal care

This chapter explains the antenatal care you'll receive and explores some of the decisions you might need to make, such as where to give birth and which tests to have. It also shows how your baby grows inside you month by month

Choosing antenatal care

Whether you opt to give birth in hospital or decide to have a home birth, most of your antenatal care will be provided by midwives, with support from your doctor and other specialists

THE TERM ANTENATAL means before birth. Whoever provides your antenatal care will perform all of the important routine check-ups that take place throughout your pregnancy. Arrangements for antenatal care vary around the country – how much choice you have depends on where you live.

Types of care

● Team care: in many places, your antenatal care will be provided by a team of midwives who will also deliver your baby in hospital (or at home or in a midwifery unit), with additional medical help being provided if necessary. Depending on how large the team is, you may or may not have met the midwife who'll be delivering you before you arrive at hospital.

● Domino scheme: a few hospitals run these schemes. When you go into labour, a midwife whom you've already met will come to your home, assist you in the early stages of labour and then accompany you to hospital and help deliver you. If the delivery is straightforward, you will be discharged to go home a few hours later.

● Midwife unit: these units may be part of a hospital or completely separate. They're

Midwives specialise in caring for pregnant women and in delivering and caring for newborn babies. To qualify, they undertake three years' training in midwifery; alternatively, they may be qualified nurses who have undertaken further training. While you are pregnant, it will probably be a midwife who performs your routine checks (see pages 42-43).

Your midwife will also let you know about antenatal classes and be able to answer any questions you have about your pregnancy and about giving birth. **Your GP** may provide your antenatal care. If your care is being provided by midwives, they will refer you to your doctor if you are experiencing any problems with your pregnancy.

Consultant obstetricians are senior doctors who specialise in the care of pregnant women. If you're having a hospital birth, you will be under the care of a consultant and his/her team. However, if your pregnancy goes well, you may not see your consultant at all. He/she will only get involved in your care if either you or your baby has problems.

Your antenatal team

managed by midwives and aim to offer a low-intervention-style birth – a bit like a home birth but in a hospital setting.

● Caseload care: this option is available in very few areas. It means you have the same two midwives throughout your pregnancy, during delivery and after the birth. If caseload midwifery isn't available in your area, you could book private care with an independent midwife (see page 168).

Giving birth in hospital

In Britain, around 95 per cent of women give birth in hospital. The advantages are:
● You may find the medical environment of the hospital reassuring.
● Help is on hand if complications occur.

● You will have access to a greater choice of pain relief, including epidurals.

The disadvantages of a hospital birth are:
● You may find the clinical environment of the hospital unnerving. It is certainly less personal than your home.
● You may have less control over what happens to you. For example, your ideas about how you would like to give birth may not be the same as those of the hospital staff.
● You're more likely to have medical intervention, such as an episiotomy (see page 70).

Giving birth at home

In 1993, a government consultation paper, 'Changing Childbirth', recommended that it should be easier for women expecting a normal delivery to have a home birth. If you want a home birth, talk to your midwife or doctor. If your pregnancy is progressing well, he/she may be positive, although some GPs don't advise home births for first babies. A home birth is also unlikely to be suitable if you have health problems, if there have been complications during your pregnancy or they are expected at the birth.

If your GP isn't keen on you having your baby at home, and there's no clear reason why you shouldn't, contact the supervisor of midwives at your local hospital or your local health authority for details of doctors who are supportive of home births. The advantages of giving birth at home are:
● Being in a familiar environment may help you to feel more relaxed and less stressed

during labour than you might feel in the more clinical surroundings of a hospital.

● It's easier to do what you want at home than in hospital. If you want to eat, watch a video or use a birthing pool, you can.

● Women who give birth at home have less medical intervention than those giving birth in hospital (although this may be due partly to the fact that women who are expected to have difficult labours are discouraged from having a home birth).

The disadvantages are:

● A home birth may not be suitable if you are expecting more than one baby.

● You will have less choice of medical pain relief – for example, you won't be able to have an epidural.

● If complications occur, it may be necessary to transfer you to hospital during labour.

● You may need to be quite determined to arrange a home birth, since availability and the medical attitude towards them varies greatly throughout the country.

Antenatal classes

Antenatal classes aim to prepare you for giving birth and for life with a new baby. Research shows that pregnant women who understand what happens during birth are more relaxed and experience less pain.

Antenatal classes have other spin-offs too, such as the chance to make new friends. Some classes are designed for couples, others just for women. Your GP or midwife should have a list of what's available locally.

Hospital/NHS classes Often called parentcraft classes, these are free and start around the 30th week (although if you are expecting a multiple birth you may be advised to start earlier). The classes are usually led by a midwife, although she may invite other health professionals along. You'll learn about pregnancy, birth and the early days with a new baby, and about what pain relief and care is available at the hospital where you're having your baby.

NCT classes The National Childbirth Trust (NCT) is Britain's largest voluntary organisation concerned with pregnancy, childbirth and the early days of life with a baby. Classes, which you pay for, are held in small groups and tend to be more in-depth than NHS classes. The NCT also provides support after birth, with groups for new mums, advice on breast-feeding, counselling for postnatal depression, and social events. Contact the NCT for more information (see page 169).

Other antenatal classes There are other classes available, such as those based on yoga or positions for pregnancy and birth. These cover similar ground to other classes, but emphasise the use of different positions in labour to reduce pain and help the birthing process along, and there's more discussion of complementary therapies. Aquanatal classes (exercise in water) are also available in some parts of the country.

Routine check-ups

Regular check-ups with your midwives or doctor give them the chance to track the progress of your pregnancy month by month and eventually, as the birth approaches, week by week

THE MOST IMPORTANT PART of antenatal care is the check-ups that begin at around 12 weeks. In most cases, these will confirm that your pregnancy is progressing normally. If any problems do develop, the checks should pick them up at an early stage so that treatment can be arranged. Because these checks are so important, you are legally entitled to time off work, including travelling time, to attend them.

Your first appointment

Your first appointment may take place at hospital or at your health centre, depending on who is providing your antenatal care. Alternatively, a team of community midwives may come to your home. Your doctor or midwife will ask about your general health, your medical history and whether this is your first pregnancy (and about any previous pregnancies or miscarriages). If you have an ongoing health problem, do mention it to your doctor.

On your first visit, you should have the chance to discuss any worries about your pregnancy and to find out about your options for giving birth (see pages 38-40).

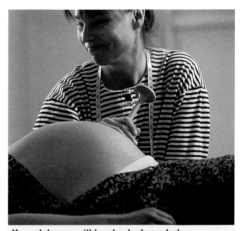

Your abdomen will be checked regularly

Routine checks

At your antenatal check-ups, your doctor or midwife will perform several tests.

Abdomen The doctor or midwife will examine your abdomen to feel how high the fundus (top of the womb) is. This gives a good idea of how far your pregnancy has progressed. If there seems to be a discrepancy between the size of the baby and how far into the pregnancy you are, you may be offered an early scan to find out, for example, if you are carrying twins.

Urine This test can check for: bacteria, which may be a sign of an infection needing treatment; sugar (glucose), which is sometimes a sign of gestational diabetes (see page 55); protein, which may indicate a risk of pre-eclampsia (see page 56) or an infection.

Weight gain This is measured routinely in parts of the country and not in others. However, if you were underweight or over-weight when you became pregnant, or seem to be putting on a great deal of weight or very little weight, you may be weighed at each check-up.

Baby's heartbeat At each one of your antenatal appointments, your midwife or doctor will probably listen to your baby's heart, using a stethoscope or a device called a doppler, which enables you to hear the heartbeat too.

Blood pressure This often rises a little during pregnancy, but if it rises a great deal, it may be a sign of pre-eclampsia (see page 56). Swelling (known as oedema) can also

Your record card

Each time you attend one of your regular check-ups, the progress of your pregnancy will be noted on your record card. Carry this with you, especially towards the end of your pregnancy, in case you have to go into hospital unexpectedly. Here's what some of the notes mean:

Date: Date of antenatal visit
Weeks: Estimate of how many weeks pregnant you are, from date of last period
LMP: Last menstrual period
BP: Blood pressure
FHH: Fetal heart heard
FMF: Fetal movement felt
Urine: NAD: nothing abnormal detected
Height of fundus: Measuring how high up the top of your womb is indicates how many weeks pregnant you are.
Presentation: C or Ceph or Vx (vertex): head down. Br (breech): bottom down
Hb: Haemoglobin, to check that you are not anaemic
E or Eng: Baby's head has engaged, i.e. descended into the pelvis, and is no longer movable
EDD: Estimated date of delivery.

be an early warning sign for pre-eclampsia, so your ankles and wrists will also be checked at each appointment.

Blood tests These test for: rhesus negative blood (see pages 56-57); anaemia, for which you will be given iron supplements; immunity to rubella (german measles), which can damage a baby if caught in pregnancy. You may also be offered tests for syphilis, hepatitis B, HIV and inherited diseases, such as thalassaemia.

How your baby grows

From the moment of conception, amazing changes are taking place inside your body – week by week, your baby is slowly developing into a recognisable human being

THE NINE MONTHS OF PREGNANCY can be roughly divided into three trimesters of around 12 weeks each. The first trimester is when all your baby's major organs develop, the second is one of rapid growth and, during the third, your baby prepares for birth.

The first three months

Weeks 0-6

You Although pregnancy is dated by doctors from the first day of your last period, conception generally takes place around two weeks after this. Some women seem to know they're pregnant instinctively; others notice that their breasts feel heavy or tingle, or that their sense of smell is extra keen. But for most women the first concrete evidence is normally a missed period.

The placenta is the organ that links your body to your baby's. Fully grown by the 12th week of pregnancy, it is attached to the wall of the womb and receives 600ml (1 pint) of blood a minute. It has two main roles: to produce hormones that help sustain the pregnancy in the early stages; and to absorb nutrients from the mother's blood and get rid of waste products from the baby's blood. It also provides a barrier to unwanted substances and infection.

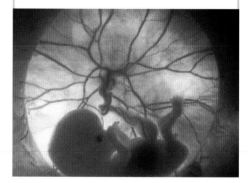

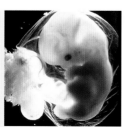

The internal organs have already begun to form in this six-week-old embryo, which is around 15mm (½in) long and floats in a sac of amniotic fluid

Your baby Probably before you realise you're pregnant, important changes are taking place inside you. After conception, the fertilised egg moves down the fallopian tube until it gets to the womb. By day seven, it has burrowed into the lining of the womb, and starts to grow. Already, the umbilical cord is starting to form. This connects your baby to your placenta (see left) and is his lifeline until the cord is cut at birth.

Weeks 6-10

You By now your period will be late and you may have already carried out a home pregnancy test. These are normally very accurate and can be used from the day your period was due. You may be experiencing morning sickness (see pages 26-27) and your breasts may feel heavy and tender.

Your baby Your baby, known at this stage as an embryo, is not much bigger than a pea and floats inside a bag of fluid. But his nervous system and brain are already forming, as well as other major organs, including the lungs, kidneys, liver and digestive system. If you had an ultrasound scan now, it would show that your baby's heart is already beating.

At around six weeks, it is possible to identify small dents on the embryo's 'head' – these will become your baby's eyes and ears. By week six, the face starts to form. By the ninth week, there are the beginnings of a mouth and tongue. Arms and legs are visible, with slight gaps where fingers and toes will be. By the end of the eighth week, your baby gets a name change, becoming known as a fetus.

Weeks 10-15

You You may have a small, distinct bump now, although for lots of women this doesn't appear until later. Your breasts are growing and your nipples are becoming darker.

Your baby This is a time of rapid growth for the fetus as all its organs and muscles become fully formed. By the end of the 12th week of pregnancy, your baby will have all his organs. His bones

At eight weeks, you won't look noticeably pregnant

and spine are formed and his sex organs are starting to develop. He has muscles, limbs and tiny finger and toenails. Your baby can now make a fist and starts to practise moving, although you won't feel anything yet. He also starts to suck, an action that will be very important in the first few months after birth. Although he's fully formed, your baby is only the size of a large satsuma.

The middle three months

Weeks 15-20

You For many women, the second three months are the most enjoyable part of pregnancy. Morning sickness usually starts to ease, the intense tiredness goes and you do not yet feel too heavy (although you may find that you sweat more). Many women have a neat bump by this time. A dark line of pigmentation, called the linea nigra, may appear down the centre of your stomach. It can be up to 1cm (⅜in) wide and stretches from the pubic hair to the naval, or even up to the breastbone. This will fade after birth.

By 19 weeks, your baby's hands are fully formed, with nails, and can curl up and make fists

Your baby Over the coming weeks, your baby will develop a distinct neck and start to grow hair, eyelashes and eyebrows. Tiny teeth start to form inside his gums. The sex organs continue to develop and an ultrasound scan may reveal what sex your baby is. In baby girls, the eggs that they will need

Expecting more than one

Around one in 105 pregnancies results in twins, and one in 10,000 in triplets. However, the incidence of multiple births is increasing as a result of fertility treatment.
Identical twins develop when one fertilised egg splits into two. Two babies grow sharing a single placenta – they will be the same sex and share the same genetic make-up and features.
Non-identical (fraternal) twins develop when two separate eggs are fertilised by two separate sperm. The babies have separate placentas, may not be the same sex and will look different from each other.
If you're expecting twins or more, you'll need more rest and will probably need to stop work sooner than if you were carrying only one baby.

for their own pregnancies in many years' time are already developing and by birth will be fully formed. At this stage, your baby's skin is very thin and transparent. If your surgery has a doppler device, you may be able to hear your baby's heartbeat at your antenatal check – it's much faster than yours. You may also feel his first feathery kicks, like a butterfly fluttering inside you.

Week 20-24

You You are probably feeling really pregnant now, as your body continues to grow steadily. Your ligaments start to soften to allow your baby to pass through your pelvis at birth. This makes your back vulnerable to injury, so you need to start taking special care of it (see pages 18-19). You're probably more aware now of when your baby's resting and when he's active.

Your baby Your baby's bones are getting harder and thicker, and his face has distinct features, although his eyelids remain closed. Your baby may be trying out facial expressions, such as frowning, and opening and closing his mouth. At around this time he becomes coated in a layer of fine hairs known as lanugo. This disappears shortly after birth. A greasy substance called vernix covers your baby and protects his skin as he floats in amniotic fluid.

Weeks 24-28

You Your shape shows beyond doubt that you're pregnant and you may put on weight in a sudden spurt, if you haven't already done so. Your breasts continue to grow and the veins may become prominent.

Your baby Once you reach the 24th week of pregnancy, your baby becomes 'viable'. This means he would have

> By 20 weeks, you'll start to become aware of your baby moving

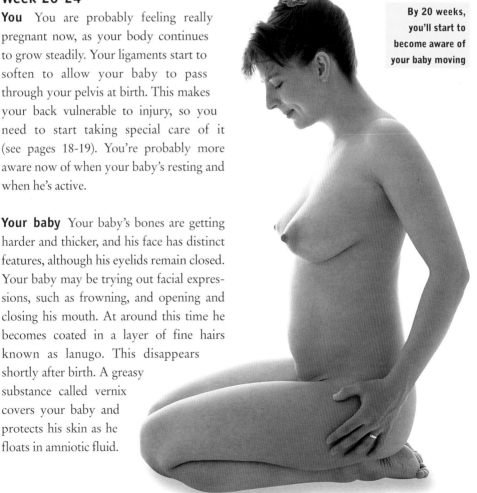

some chance of survival if he were born now (known as being born prematurely). However, the closer to maturity your baby is born, the better his chances.

Your baby's hearing is developing and he will find the voices, and even the music, that he hears now soothing, once he is born. Around week 26, his eyelids open. Your baby's heart is now beating so strongly that it can be heard with a stethoscope. You may even feel him hiccuping, a strange rhythmic jumping which is nothing to worry about. Your baby now weighs just a bit more than a bag of sugar.

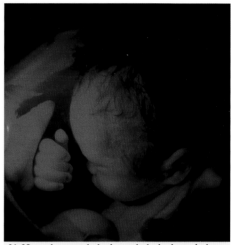

At 40 weeks, your baby is ready to be born, but he's unlikely to arrive exactly on his due date

The last three months

Weeks 28-32

You With your baby gaining weight rapidly during these weeks, the size of your bump increases significantly, perhaps making you feel breathless or tired. The skin on your abdomen becomes very stretched and stretchmarks may start to appear on your stomach and thighs. Your breasts may begin to produce colostrum, a watery substance that provides your baby with important nourishment in the first days after birth. You may find your breasts leak a little.

Your baby Your baby's lungs are maturing, although he might still need help with breathing if he were born now. He can distinguish between light and dark, and his taste buds are working. Up until now your baby has been rather scrawny, but the fat stores he has been developing in recent weeks – and will continue to develop – make him much more rounded. But he still has lots of growing to do. If he were born now, he would weigh not much more than half what he would weigh at full term.

Your baby is becoming fairly cramped in your womb. He is curled up and less able to move freely, although when he does move it's more noticeable. By about week 32, most babies will have turned head down (cephalic) ready for birth, but a few remain with their bottom at the bottom of the womb and their head at the top (breech). Some breech babies turn before the birth, but others remain in this position and may need extra care during delivery or possibly a caesarean delivery (see page 74).

Weeks 32-36

You As your growing womb puts pressure on your bladder (and indeed on all your other organs), you may find you need to go to the loo all the time. This, and your size and shape, can make getting a good night's sleep difficult. Some women experience mild, irregular practice contractions known as Braxton-Hicks. If these contractions become strong and regular, talk to your midwife in case you're starting labour (see page 66). Be aware that twins often arrive earlier than single babies.

Your baby Your baby continues to prod with his elbows and give little kicks, although space is getting really tight now. By now, he weighs over 2kg (about 4lbs 6oz). His head may drop down into your pelvis, ready for birth (engagement), giving you a strange sensation, called lightening, when you walk. Some babies don't engage until labour begins – this is more common in women who've had babies before.

Week 36-40

You By now, you may feel huge, cumbersome and increasingly impatient. Even if sleep is difficult, it's important to get as much rest as possible. For most women, labour starts some time after week 36 or in the week after their due date – only five per cent of women give birth on their due date. Shortly before their baby arrives, many women experience a nesting instinct – a desire to get their home clean and tidy, ready for the baby.

Your baby Each day your baby puts on another 30g (1oz), though his weight gain will slow down as the delivery gets closer. Like you, your baby is just waiting for the big day to arrive.

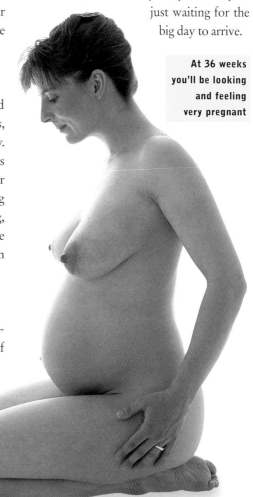

At 36 weeks you'll be looking and feeling very pregnant

Scans and tests

Modern screening techniques can provide your antenatal care team with a great deal of information about your baby and how he's developing – even while he's still inside you

ANTENATAL TESTS ARE USED for a number of purposes – to find out, for example, whether the placenta is in the right position, whether your baby is growing normally or even if your baby has a chromosomal disorder. Some of the problems that can be identified, such as cleft palate, may be treatable; others, such as Down's syndrome and spina bifida, are not. There are two types of test: screening tests and diagnostic tests.

Screening tests

The advantage of screening tests (also known as risk tests) is that, because they consist of either blood tests or scans, they won't cause any harm to your baby. The disadvantage is that they cannot tell you for certain whether your baby has a particular condition, only whether your risk is higher or lower than normal. If your risk is high, you may be offered a diagnostic test, which can give you a definite answer.

Ultrasound scans Ultrasound is the most common screening test in the early stages of pregnancy and, for many couples, watching their baby on the screen is one of the highlights of pregnancy. For many men, in particular, it's the first time the baby actually seems real. You may even be given a print-out of the image you see on screen to take home with you.

Ultrasound works by using soundwaves to build up a picture of the baby inside the womb. Unlike X-rays, this type of scan does not emit radiation and is harmless to both you and your baby.

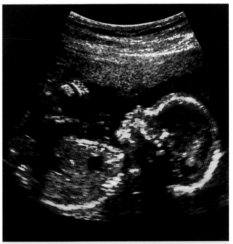

Seeing your baby on a scan for the first time is one of the highlights of pregnancy and can reassure you that your baby is developing normally

developing properly. It can also be used to identify whether the baby is at risk of Down's syndrome or has a heart or limb malformation. If your radiographer spots a problem, you'll be referred to a consultant who will be able to tell you more and who may suggest further tests.

You may be offered more scans later in your pregnancy, if you are expecting twins or if you're overdue, for example. As with all tests, you are perfectly entitled to refuse an ultrasound if you do not want one.

What happens in a scan? Scans take place at the hospital and you can bring a partner or friend along with you if you like. You may be asked to drink a pint of liquid shortly before arriving at the hospital and not to go to the toilet until after the scan. This is because a full bladder helps give a better picture on older machines. However, rather than facing a long drive on a full bladder, it might be a better idea to take along a bottle of water with you and drink it before your appointment.

Once in the consulting room, you'll be asked to lie on a couch. The radiographer will spread a jelly-like substance over your bare stomach and then pass an instrument across it, which is painless. As the instrument is moved backwards and forwards

When will I have one? In some areas, women are offered a dating scan at around eight to 13 weeks. This establishes when the baby is due and whether there's just one baby or more. You may also be offered an early scan if you have vaginal bleeding, extreme morning sickness or if you've had fertility treatment.

At around 16-20 weeks of pregnancy, all women should be offered a scan known as an anomaly scan. As well as checking the baby's growth and its position, and the position of the placenta, this scan is used to check whether the brain and spine are

The radiographer will spread a jelly-like substance over your bare stomach and pass an instrument across it

you'll be able to see a picture of your baby on a screen. Sometimes the operator will talk you through the scan.

A scan at 16-20 weeks can identify the sex of your baby with a fair degree of accuracy. Some hospitals will tell you the sex if you ask, others have a policy of not telling. If it is important for you to know – or not to know – the sex of your baby, explain this to the operator beforehand.

Alpha fetoprotein (AFP) This is a blood test which measures levels of a certain protein (AFP) to find out if you have a high or low risk of carrying a baby with spina bifida or Down's syndrome. It's performed at around 16-18 weeks of pregnancy and is about 66 per cent accurate (it identifies two

out of every three cases). The triple/quadruple/Bart's blood test is slightly more accurate and also gives a risk factor for several other conditions. It isn't always offered routinely so you may have to ask for it.

Nuchal fold test This is a fairly new ultrasound scan which is performed on a top-quality machine at ten to 14 weeks. By measuring the thickness of skin folds around the baby's neck, the operator can predict the likelihood of a baby having Down's syndrome. The test is over 80 per cent accurate, but is only available in certain hospitals on the NHS, although you can get one done privately. If the nuchal fold test shows a high risk of Down's syndrome, you'll be offered an amniocentesis.

To **test** or not to **test**

Although tests can answer many questions, they can also cause a great deal of anxiety. If you have a screening test and are found to have a 'high' risk, you will have to decide whether to have a diagnostic test, which increases the risk of miscarriage. If you have amniocentesis, for instance, you'll face a worrying wait of two weeks or more before you know if your baby has – or does not have – Down's syndrome. If you do have a diagnostic test, you'll breathe a huge sigh of relief

if you find out your baby is fine. On the other hand, if a problem is discovered, then you'll face a stark and very personal choice. Before you have any tests, ask yourself the following questions:
• How would I feel about having a child with, say, Down's syndrome? Could I love and cope with that child or would I prefer a termination?
• What is my attitude to abortion? Would I want to carry on with my pregnancy whatever disability was found?

• If I wouldn't terminate, how do I feel about testing? Would knowing I was carrying a handicapped child spoil the rest of my pregnancy or would I want to be prepared?
If a test shows that your baby has a major problem, support is available from Antenatal Results and Choices (see page 168). If you decide to continue with the pregnancy knowing you'll have a child with special needs, there are support groups who can help (see pages 168-169).

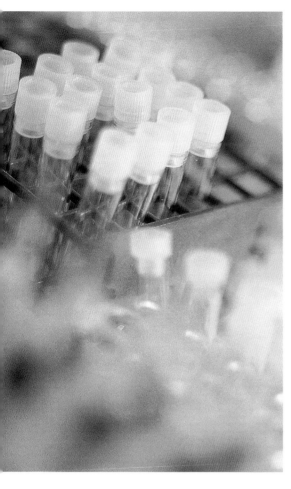

Diagnostic tests

The advantage of diagnostic tests is that they can tell you definitely whether your baby is suffering from a certain condition or not. The disadvantage is that they involve putting something into the womb, which means there is an increased risk of miscarriage afterwards.

Diagnostic tests are normally only offered to women who have already had a scan or blood test showing that they have a higher risk factor than normal of carrying a baby with a chromosomal disorder. They are also offered to women with a family history of chromosome disorders.

Amniocentesis This test is performed after 16 weeks of pregnancy. It involves inserting a needle into the womb, under local anaesthetic, and withdrawing amniotic fluid for testing. The results take two or more weeks to come through. On average, one in every 100 women who undergo amniocentesis will have a miscarriage. However, some consultants may have a lower ratio and others higher. The use of continuously guided ultrasound reduces the chance of miscarriage, so make certain that you are referred to a centre that uses this.

Chorionic villus sampling (CVS) This is an alternative to amniocentesis, offered at around 12 weeks of pregnancy. The doctor takes a small sample of tissue from the placenta, either through a needle inserted directly into the womb or through the entrance to the womb. This is tested and the results given in about ten days. The advantage of this test is that it takes place so early in the pregnancy. However, nationally, there is a slightly higher risk of miscarriage than with amniocentesis, though much depends on the skill of the operator.

Cordocentesis This test is performed on blood drawn from the umbilical cord at around 20 weeks and can identify some conditions that amniocentesis and CVS cannot. However, it's only available in certain centres. The risk of miscarriage is slightly higher than for other tests.

Possible complications

Most pregnancies progress normally, but if complications do develop, they can often be successfully managed to give you the best possible chance of having a healthy baby

VERY OCCASIONALLY, things go wrong in pregnancy, but there are usually warning signs that allow the problem to be dealt with before you or your baby are put at risk.

Anaemia

During pregnancy, your body needs to manufacture more blood cells than usual, both for you and for the healthy development of your baby. If you're deficient in iron, which is vital for the production of blood cells, you may become anaemic.

Anaemia is thinning of the blood, which causes tiredness, pale skin and breathlessness, and can lower resistance to infection. Teenagers, women expecting more than one baby and those who've had a baby in the previous year are at particular risk. Anaemia is common in menstruating women and one in seven women is anaemic before becoming pregnant.

All pregnant women are checked for anaemia through a routine blood test. You can help prevent it by eating more iron-rich food during pregnancy (see page 11). If you are anaemic, your doctor may prescribe iron tablets and suggest changes to your diet.

Ectopic pregnancy

An ectopic pregnancy occurs when a fertilised egg implants outside the womb, generally in the fallopian tube. It's a dangerous condition because, as the embryo grows, it starts to place pressure on the tube and surrounding organs. Left untreated, an ectopic pregnancy can be life-threatening.

Around one in 100 pregnancies is ectopic, but it's a difficult condition to diagnose. First symptoms generally occur before the tenth week of pregnancy and include low, one-sided and sometimes intense stomach

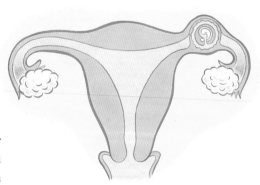

In an ectopic pregnancy, the embryo implants in the fallopian tube instead of the womb

About one in five of all pregnancies ends in miscarriage (losing the baby before the 24th week of pregnancy). The vast majority of miscarriages occur before nine weeks, sometimes before a woman realises she's pregnant.

The first signs of miscarriage are bleeding and cramps. At other times, a scan may show that the baby has died. If you have a miscarriage at home, you may be sent for a check-up to be sure that your womb is empty. If it isn't, you may be advised to undergo a short operation. If a miscarriage has not started, but the baby is dead, you may be offered an operation to remove the baby or tablets to speed up miscarriage. However, some women prefer to wait for the miscarriage to take place naturally.

After a miscarriage, it is natural to feel a host of emotions: grief, anger, depression, emptiness or isolation. Sometimes friends may not understand your pain and will try to help by reminding you that you can have another baby or by encouraging you to move on with your life. However, grief in this situation is entirely normal and you will need time and support to help you recover.

The next pregnancy usually progresses without any problems. If you're among the few women who have recurrent miscarriages, ask to be referred to a specialist centre. For more information, contact the Miscarriage Association (see page 169).

pain, possibly with vaginal bleeding, often dark and watery. There may be pain on moving the bowels or in the shoulder tips. If you have any of these symptoms, contact your GP immediately.

If your doctor suspects an ectopic pregnancy, he'll refer you to hospital for an ultrasound scan or laparoscopy (viewing of the fallopian tubes). It may be possible to remove the embryo without removing the fallopian tube, but in some cases the tube may need to be surgically removed. Although your chances of conceiving are lower after an ectopic pregnancy, many women go on to conceive normally.

Losing a baby through ectopic pregnancy can be traumatic. If you would like to talk to someone who knows how it feels, contact the Miscarriage Association (see page 169).

Gestational diabetes

Sometimes pregnancy triggers diabetes in women who have never previously had the condition. So-called gestational diabetes occurs when the demands of the pregnancy exceed the ability of the hormone insulin to control blood sugar levels. Generally, the condition is discovered through urine testing at antenatal checks, but other symptoms include intense thirst, thrush, blurred vision and producing large quantities of urine at frequent intervals.

Gestational diabetes generally disappears after the birth, but if you're affected, you'll need to take special care about what and when you eat throughout pregnancy. You may need to monitor your glucose levels – your doctor will advise on this – and some women may need insulin injections.

Placenta praevia

Placenta praevia occurs when the placenta positions itself lower than normal in the womb, over or near the cervix. This happens in around one in 200 pregnancies. The first symptom is often painless bleeding in the final months of pregnancy. Provided the bleeding isn't too heavy, you'll probably be advised to rest, although more severe cases may need to stay in hospital until the baby is delivered. A caesarean is usually necessary as a low-lying placenta will become detached early in labour, cutting the baby's oxygen supply and causing problems for the mother.

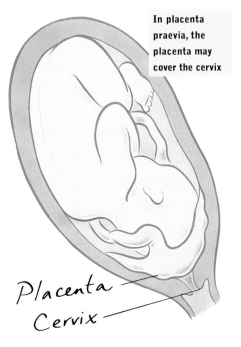

In placenta praevia, the placenta may cover the cervix

Placenta
Cervix

Pre-eclampsia

Pre-eclampsia is one of the most common complications in pregnancy, affecting one in ten women to some degree, although most cases are mild. It's more likely to occur in a first pregnancy and is thought to be caused by an abnormality in the placenta, although it may not become apparent until late in pregnancy. Pre-eclampsia may mean that your baby grows slowly, but the condition is particularly dangerous for the mother as, left untreated, it can cause damage to the kidneys and liver, convulsions and even death.

Pre-eclampsia cannot be prevented and there's no way of predicting who will be affected. However, it can be detected by testing urine, checking for swelling and monitoring blood pressure, which is why these tests are carried out at every antenatal check. First symptoms of pre-eclampsia may include severe swelling of hands, face

or feet, pain just under the ribs, a bad headache, vomiting, blurred vision and spots in front of the eyes. If you have any of these symptoms, contact your doctor or midwife. If you have pre-eclampsia, your medical team will decide if and when labour needs to be induced, as the condition only improves once the baby has been delivered.

Contact Action on Pre-Eclampsia for more information (see page 168).

Rhesus incompatibility

A woman with a rhesus negative blood group can form antibodies to her baby if he is rhesus positive. This is unlikely to cause problems in a first pregnancy and, for subsequent pregnancies, can be prevented by special injections called anti-D. These are given after birth to rhesus negative women and may also be given during pregnancy in some centres.

Small for dates babies

Your midwife will monitor your baby's growth by measuring the distance from your pelvic bone to the top of your womb. If your baby seems unusually large or small, she may suggest an ultrasound. This will help establish whether the baby is actually due on the date originally calculated. If your due date proves to be accurate, your baby is said to be small (or large) for dates.

Your baby may be small for dates if you are a smoker, undernourished, ill or have an ongoing medical condition. If you smoke or aren't eating properly, your doctor can advise you on giving up smoking and improving your diet (see pages 8-15). If you've been ill, you may be given treatment that is safe for your baby and advised to rest for a while. You will also be carefully monitored to see how your baby is progressing.

Your baby may be large for dates if you have diabetes or are very overweight. You'll be closely monitored and may have an induction or caesarean if your baby is too large for a normal birth at full term.

Vaginal bleeding

In the early months of pregnancy, vaginal bleeding can occur for a number of reasons. In the majority of cases, the pregnancy

Stillbirth

A stillbirth occurs when a baby is born dead after the 24th week of pregnancy. Although stillbirth is rare, it's devastating for the parents involved who, instead of greeting their baby, find themselves saying goodbye. There are many causes of stillbirth and sometimes no apparent reason for the baby dying.

If you lose your baby, both you and your partner will need support to deal with the grief, anger and loss you may feel – you may want to contact an organisation for bereaved parents such as SANDS (see page 169). Years ago, parents whose baby was stillborn were expected to carry on as if nothing had happened. We now know that this isn't helpful and that parents must be allowed to grieve. You may want to arrange a funeral for the baby or to have keepsakes, such as a photo.

If you're pregnant again after having experienced a stillbirth, it's natural to feel a mix of happiness and sadness, and to worry about what might go wrong. You may find it helpful to talk to your health team about your fears.

continues normally, but sometimes it's a sign of a threatened miscarriage or ectopic pregnancy, particularly if accompanied by abdominal pain. It's therefore vital to contact your doctor if you start to bleed.

Later on in the pregnancy, bleeding may be a sign that the placenta is positioned lower than normal (placenta praevia) or is coming away (placental abruption). If this happens, your doctor may suggest a scan to confirm the diagnosis, followed by bed rest and perhaps hospitalisation.

Your baby is born

No two births are ever
the same but every one
of them is extraordinary.
This chapter explains what
happens when a baby
is born and helps you
prepare for giving birth

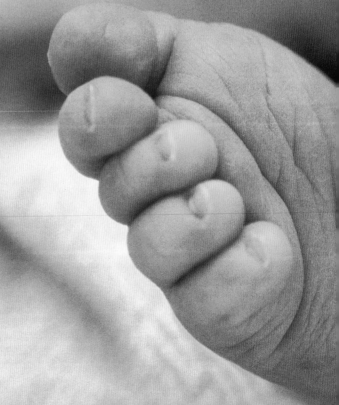

Countdown to labour

As your due date draws closer, you'll need to make the final preparations for your baby's arrival. From writing your birth plan to arranging postnatal help, there's plenty to think about

THE EXPERIENCE OF GIVING BIRTH differs greatly for everyone and the sort of labour you will have is determined largely by the size and position of your baby and the shape of your pelvis. But, if you are about to give birth for the first time, you probably have one feeling in common with all first-time mothers – apprehension. This is completely normal. However, research shows that the more information a woman has about the process of giving birth and the more she feels she has a say in what happens during the labour and delivery, the better she is able to cope.

Writing your birth plan

Writing a birth plan gives you the chance to think about your options for the birth and to express a preference. However, you should be aware that things may need to change – for example, if your baby is distressed, if you find the pain difficult to bear or if there are complications.

It's more important that you and your baby emerge safely and positively from the delivery than that you stick to your birth plan.

Make sure your birth partner knows that the birth plan can be adapted, too. There is no point you begging your medical or midwifery staff for pain relief while your birth partner is telling them you don't want any because it says so on the birth plan.

Use your birth plan to talk through your preferences with your midwife when you arrive at the hospital. Points to cover in your plan include:

- Who do I want with me? My partner, my mother or someone else? Do I want them there all the time? Do I want them there if I have a forceps delivery or caesarean?
- Do I want to be able to move about, have a bath or use a birthing pool?
- How would I feel about medical or midwifery students being present?
- Do I want medical pain relief and, if so, what kind? (See page 65.)

- How do I feel about the possibility of having an episiotomy? (See page 70.)
- Am I planning to breast-feed my baby? (See pages 104-109.)
- Do I want my baby handed straight to me after she's born, or cleaned up first?
- Do I want to have syntometrine to help me deliver the placenta quickly or would I prefer to deliver it naturally? (See page 70.)
- How do I feel about my baby being given vitamin K? (See page 71.)
- Do I have any special requirements (such as religious customs that I observe or other special needs) that midwifery or medical staff should know about in advance?

Your birth partner

Having someone with you to comfort and support you through labour can actually help to make giving birth easier. If you have a husband or partner, he may well be your natural choice as a birth partner. Your mother, a sister or a good friend can all be a good choice, too.

Most men welcome the opportunity to see the start of their new baby's life and support the woman they love through birth. If this applies to your partner, the best way he can help you is by going along to antenatal classes with you. It's important that he knows what to expect so he can discuss your birth plan and provide you with support on the big day.

However, being in on the birth isn't for all men. Some feel that seeing their lover giving birth may affect their sexual relationship; others are squeamish or simply can't guarantee to be able to make it when the day arrives due to work commitments (this can happen even if your partner planned to be there, as only one in 20 babies arrives on her due date). If your partner really doesn't want to be there, it's best not to force him. After all, you don't want to have to worry about him as well as the baby.

Some men compromise, accompanying their partner to the hospital and then going home and returning after the birth. In the event that your partner cannot be with you, for whatever reason, choose another birth partner to provide support.

Practical preparations

By week 36 of your pregnancy, you should be prepared not just for the birth, but for bringing your baby home, too. Check that you have made the following preparations:

- Informed your employer of planned maternity leave in writing
- Packed your hospital and baby bag
- Written your birth plan
- Put the telephone numbers of the hospital and midwife in a handy place
- Filled the car up with petrol and saved enough change for hospital parking charges
- Fitted a baby car seat and checked that you know how to use it
- Asked your partner/mum/friends to help out once you and your baby are home
- Stocked the freezer and store cupboard for after the birth.

Your hospital bag
- Maternity notes and birth plan
- Baggy, long, cotton T-shirt or night dress, preferably old, for giving birth
- Socks and warm top for after the birth or in case you feel very cold
- Toiletry bag containing soap, shampoo, toothbrush, toothpaste, deodorant, flannel and a hairbrush or comb
- Massage lotion
- Water spray to cool you down
- Water or juice to drink during labour
- Glucose tablets for energy
- Snack for your birth partner
- Cassette player and soothing music
- Coins or phonecard (mobile phones will not be permitted in hospital because they interfere with medical equipment)
- Camera and film
- Dressing gown and a pair of slippers for wearing on the ward after the birth
- Two front-opening nightdresses and two maternity bras, if you are planning to breast-feed your baby
- At least 24 maternity pads for after the birth and two packs of disposable pants
- Breast pads for absorbing leaks
- Coming-home outfit (don't forget that you'll still be bigger than you were before you became pregnant).

Your baby bag
- Pack of nappies (newborn size)
- Cotton wool for cleaning your baby
  - Three sleepsuits (newborn size)
    - Three vests (newborn size)
      - Shawl/blanket, hat and gloves for when you take your baby home (particularly if the weather is very cold).

Help after the birth

The first few weeks with a new baby can be demanding. As well as learning to care for your new baby, you will also be recovering from the birth and trying to adjust to the enormous changes that motherhood brings. And all of this on top of much less sleep than you are used to.

Getting support is crucial during these early weeks. If you are expecting twins, support will be, quite literally, doubly important. Organisations like TAMBA can provide help and advice (see page 169).

The kind of support you choose will depend largely on your own personality and environment. Here are some of the ways that others can help:

● Practical support with washing, cooking, housework and shopping is appreciated by most mums with a new baby.

● Help with your baby while you get some sleep can make a big difference. Equally, if you have older children, it's invaluable if someone they know is there to give them some extra attention.

● Moral support, such as talking through your experiences with a sympathetic friend, can give you a real boost. Beware, however, of friends and relatives who give you endless advice about the way you should be doing things. Advice that undermines your confidence or goes against what you feel is right is worse than useless. Remember that there is no single right way to look after a baby and ideas on how to care for babies have changed radically in the last 30 years. If you have a relative or friend who wants to tell you what to do, try to redirect her energies towards what she could be doing to help, such as shopping and cooking.

Your partner Research shows that the more involved a man is with his baby, the more involved a father he becomes. If your partner helps you with your baby, you can both learn what suits her, and the support you give each other will be invaluable.

Relatives Provided you get on with them and they are willing to help, relatives are another good source of support.

Maternity nurse This is a carer who specialises in looking after newborn babies. Many are qualified nurses, midwives or nursery nurses experienced in baby care. They are expensive, but are on call 24 hours a day (apart from their day off). They live with you and may be ideal if you do not have family or friends who can help out regularly, or if you are expecting twins or more. A good maternity nurse will help care for a baby, but will not monopolise her.

Mother's help A mother's help is not trained in babycare but can help you look after your baby under your supervision. She may also help with the housework.

To find a maternity nurse or mother's help, ask friends for recommendations or go through a nanny agency (look them up in your Yellow Pages). Make sure you interview candidates before the birth and take up at least two references by phone as well as in writing. See pages 144-145 for more hints on interviewing techniques.

Sources of support

Options for pain relief

If you are about to give birth for the first time, the prospect can be daunting. However, understanding the different types of pain relief available can help you feel more confident

THERE ARE MANY WAYS of managing pain during labour, from simple breathing exercises that draw the attention away from the pain, to epidurals which can make giving birth an almost pain-free experience.

Self-help options

Self-help techniques are especially useful in the early stages of labour. The advantage is that they do not involve the use of drugs, so there are no side effects for you or your baby. They help you cope with the pain, rather than taking it away. Options include:

Active birth positions These help to keep you moving – and the more mobile you are, the faster labour is likely to progress. There are positions suitable for all stages of labour and some even help the baby to move down the birth canal.

Breathing Slow breathing patterns in the early stages of labour will help you to relax, and other breathing techniques can help relieve contractions and focus attention away from the pain. For more information, ask at your antenatal class.

Complementary therapies Massage, reflexology, acupuncture, hypnosis and aromatherapy (see pages 28-29) can all help relieve pain. You will need to seek advice from practitioners well before the birth, and you'll also need hospital permission if you want a practitioner present.

TENS For some women, transcutaneous nerve stimulation (TENS) helps in coping with the pain. A hand-held machine passes tiny electric shocks to your back, via electrodes attached by pads. The shocks stimulate production of endorphins, the body's natural pain-killer, and block pain messages to the brain. It's important to start using TENS from the onset of labour for maximum effect. You can buy or hire TENS machines for use at home. Ask at your hospital or contact the National Childbirth Trust (see page 169).

Water Buoyancy makes it easier to manoeuvre and water soothes and takes the edge off contractions – this is why some women use a birthing pool. If you don't have access to one, a bath will help.

Medical pain relief

If you give birth in hospital, you will have access to a range of pain-relieving drugs. For a home birth, Entonox and, in some cases, pethidine will be available.

Entonox Often known as gas and air, this is a mixture of oxygen and nitrous oxide (laughing gas) which you breathe in through a hand-held mask. Entonox takes the edge off the pain but it doesn't remove it alto-gether. However, it can be combined with pethidine for more effective pain relief.

Spinal cord

Epidural space

● Advantages: Entonox does not harm your baby and is quickly expelled from your body once you stop using it. You are in control of how much Entonox you use.
● Disadvantages: You may dislike the feel of the mask or feel sick or dizzy. Entonox alone may not provide sufficient relief.

Pethidine This is injected into the thigh or buttocks once labour is well-established and helps reduce pain to a more manageable level. If it works well, you will find you feel relaxed or sleepy, and this can ease labour if you are very tense. The effects wear off after four hours. Some maternity units use alternatives such as meptazinol.
● Advantages: Pethidine can reduce pain without causing complete loss of sensation.

● Disadvantages: You may find that it makes you feel drowsy or nauseous. It can also make your baby sleepy or affect her breathing or urge to feed if it's given too close to delivery.

Epidural A local anaesthetic is injected into the epidural space in the lower back via a fine, hollow tube. The tube is inserted through a needle and left in place during labour so that top-up doses can be given.
● Advantages: For most women, an epidural blocks pain completely. As a result, it is often used where labour is prolonged and painful. It is also useful if there is a risk of a caesarean as the epidural can be topped up quite quickly. An epidural can lower high blood pressure.
● Disadvantages: Sometimes an epidural does not work completely or works on one side only. Some women dislike the feeling of numbness in the legs. Traditional epidu-rals prevent you from moving around in labour, which can cause things to slow down, although certain hospitals offer a mobile epidural so some movement is poss-ible. An epidural can also make pushing the baby out more difficult which makes an episiotomy and an assisted delivery more likely (see page 72). However, this can some-times be overcome by allowing time for the epidural to wear off before pushing begins.

What happens in labour

Labour falls into three stages. Understanding the changes that take place in your body at each stage will help you to work effectively with your care team as you give birth to your baby

EVERY LABOUR IS DIFFERENT. No-one can predict exactly when each one will begin, how long it will last and whether it will progress exactly as it should. Whatever happens, your care team is trained to help you and your baby come through this remarkable experience as safely as possible.

First signs of labour

There are several signs that labour is about to start. These include:

● A show: this is a clear, jelly-like discharge, stained with blood. It occurs when the mucus that seals the cervix comes away and is a sign that the cervix is softening, ready for labour. If you have any other bleeding besides a show, report it to your GP or midwife immediately.

● Your waters break: the bag of fluid that surrounds your baby may break and the amniotic fluid (your waters) will come out, either in a trickle or a gush. Contact your midwife or hospital straightaway.

● Regular contractions: you may have been having irregular, mild contractions for a few days or even weeks. When the contractions start coming steadily, say every ten minutes or less, and last between 30 seconds and one minute, contact your midwife or hospital. Get in touch with your midwife earlier if the contractions are worryingly strong or there is anything you are concerned about. Don't worry that you are being a nuisance or that it may be a false labour. Your midwife would much rather reassure you than have you fret.

What to do As the contractions start to strengthen, you may feel excited, nervous, panicky or even frightened. Now is the time to start using the self-help techniques that you practised in antenatal classes. Massage, birth positions such as resting over a bean bag, pelvic tilts and breathing exercises may all help. You may want to have a warm bath, which will help to relax you. Have a snack to keep your energy up if you feel like it, but check that it's OK with your midwife first. Try not to think about the contractions to come but take them one at a time and do your best to relax in-between each one. You may find it helps to keep on the move – it's a question of seeing what works best for you.

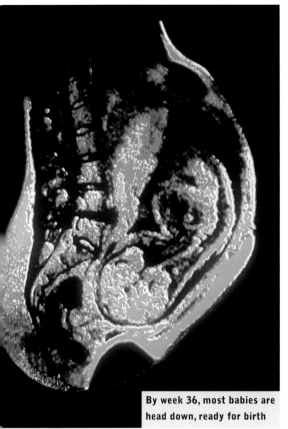

By week 36, most babies are head down, ready for birth

First stage

During the first stage of labour you'll experience contractions which become stronger as labour progresses. In a contraction, the womb muscles tighten, gradually stretching the cervix open so that the baby can pass out of the womb and into the birth canal (see below). For a first baby, it can take from as little as a few hours to as much as two days for the cervix to dilate fully to approximately 10cm.

Going to hospital Go to hospital when contractions are coming every five minutes, or sooner if you're anxious or have been told to report in at the first twinge. On admission (or at home, if you're having a home birth) your midwife will ask if your waters have broken or if you have had a show. Your blood pressure and a urine sample will be taken, your pulse checked, abdomen felt and an internal examination carried out to see how far dilated you are. At this stage, self-help techniques can be soothing, but as contractions become stronger, you may want medical pain relief, which you can discuss with your midwife (see page 65).

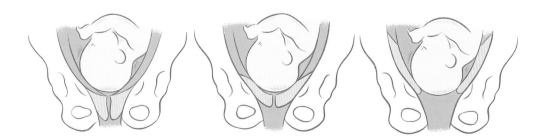

Before labour begins, hormones help soften the cervix (left). During the first stage, contractions thin and then dilate the cervix (centre). By the end of transition, the cervix has dilated to 10cm (right)

Monitoring your baby

Throughout your labour your baby's heart rate will be monitored to ensure she continues to receive adequate oxygen via the placenta. A baby's heart rate is a useful indicator to how she is coping with labour and can be used to pick up any early signs of distress. You will probably be monitored at intervals (rather than continuously) unless complications occur. There are several ways to monitor a baby.

• **A doppler** is a small ultrasound device which is held against your tummy by a midwife. Sometimes known as a sonicaid, it does not restrict movement and allows you to remain mobile.

• **A pinard stethoscope** is a traditional ear trumpet. As it is simply held against your tummy, it allows you to move freely.

• **An electronic fetal monitor (EFM)** allows your care team to monitor your baby continuously. A receiver to measure the baby's heartbeat is attached via a belt wrapped around your tummy. Sometimes, the receiver is attached to the baby's scalp via a small electrode introduced vaginally. Another receiver to measure contractions is attached via the belt around your tummy. One advantage of EFM is that you can see each contraction starting on the monitor before you feel it. The disadvantage is that you can't move around, or use a birthing pool or TENS machine. If your care team wants to monitor you continuously in this way, you may want to find out why.

• **Telemetry** uses radio waves to monitor the baby's heart rate continuously. You can usually move freely as the receivers (often strapped to your thigh) are not attached to a machine. Sometimes, electrodes are introduced vaginally and attached to the baby's scalp, but you'll still be able to move around.

Transition

This is usually the most difficult part of labour as your womb contracts to bring the cervix to full dilation (10cm), so that the baby's head can emerge. During transition, which lasts around half an hour, contractions are at their strongest and last about one minute each. They are very close together, with hardly any space to rest between them.

At this point, it's not unusual to feel that the pain is unbearable and that you want to give up. Or you may feel exhausted, nauseous, shaky, shivery, bad tempered or just fed up. Your midwife will support you through this phase – it won't be long now before your baby is born.

You may feel an urge to push. If you do, tell your midwife straight away – she will feel to see if you are sufficiently dilated. If you are not, she may suggest breathing exercises to reduce the urge to push. She may also suggest you get onto all fours, rest your head in your arms and stick your bottom up. This makes pushing more difficult.

Second stage

During the second stage of labour, strong contractions push your baby out of the womb and you'll probably feel a powerful urge to help push her out, too. For a first baby, this stage usually takes about an hour.

Your midwife will let you know when it's safe to push. She'll suggest different ways of breathing and positions to help make your

Your midwife will let you know when it's safe to push and suggest breathing and positions to make it easier

pushes more efficient, and show your birth partner how to provide encouragement. If you have had an epidural that hasn't yet worn off, you may not feel the urge to push. In this case, your midwife can show you how to time your pushes, even if you don't feel them. If this happens, you are more likely to need an assisted delivery with forceps or ventouse (see page 72).

As your baby's head starts to appear, your midwife will help you get into a good position for delivery. Some women like to squat so that gravity helps their baby to slide down. However, if by this time you are exhausted and shaky, this may not work for you and you may prefer to sit upright,

propped up with pillows and gripping your thighs. Some women prefer to kneel, to go down on all fours or to lie on their side, but if you need an assisted delivery, you may find that you have to lie on your back with your legs in stirrups.

Once the top of your baby's head becomes visible and does not slip back between contractions (this is known as 'crowning') your midwife will instruct you not to push too hard. This is to give the vaginal opening a chance to stretch gradually and helps to reduce the risk of tearing. Your midwife may also suggest breathing techniques, such as panting, to help slow down the pushes.

Delivery of twins or more requires special skills and you will normally be attended by an obstetrician, a paediatrician and possibly an anaesthetist, as well as one or more midwives. To protect you and your babies, you will all be more closely monitored than with routine births.

The position of your twins will determine what sort of a birth you have. Often a scan is taken before a 'trial of labour' is allowed. If your babies are in an awkward delivery position, your obstetrician may advise a caesarean, or you may be advised to have an epidural in case an emergency caesarean is necessary. Around half of all twins and most triplets are delivered by

caesarean. If you do have a natural birth you will have two second stages rather than one and you should be prepared to have an assisted delivery, using either forceps or ventouse (see page 72).

Twins and triplets are more likely to need special care after the birth than single babies as they may be premature and have lower birth weights (see page 80). All of this may sound daunting, but the fact that your medical team is alert to the risk of complications means that they will do everything they can to prevent them and keep you and your babies safe. For this reason, you will need to be flexible in your ideas about the sort of birth you want.

Giving birth to **twins**

Your baby is born

As the vaginal opening stretches to let the baby's head out, you'll feel a stinging sensation followed by numbness. If the midwife is worried that you may tear badly as the baby's head comes through, or if she needs to help your baby out more quickly, she tenderness towards your baby and want to take her into your arms straight away. Unless you have asked for her to be cleaned up, she may still be blood-stained or covered in vernix, the white, sticky stuff that coats a baby while she's in the womb. If you want, you can put your baby to your breast.

You may feel a great surge of tenderness towards your baby and want to take her into your arms straightaway

may ask your permission to give you an episiotomy (see box below). Then, with one contraction, your baby's head emerges; with the next contraction, the rest of her body comes sliding out.

If she's breathing well, she will normally be put on your stomach. Sometimes your partner will be invited to cut the cord, or your midwife or doctor may do this. If your baby isn't breathing well, her airways will be cleared and she may be given oxygen. At this stage, you may feel a great surge of

What is **an episiotomy?**

An episiotomy is a small, controlled cut made to enlarge the vaginal opening and help prevent tearing. It is often necessary if a baby is breech, has a big head or is distressed, or if you are having an assisted delivery (see page 72). It is usually carried out as the baby's head 'crowns' and between contractions. You'll normally be given a local anaesthetic, which may need topping up later when the cut is stitched.

Even after a very long labour, surges of hormones can leave you feeling very alert. However, you may find you're so exhausted that you just want someone else to hold the baby. This response is perfectly normal, and feeling too tired to care doesn't mean you're going to be a bad mother, merely that you've had a long or difficult delivery.

Third stage

Once you've given birth, you'll experience another contraction which will help to expel the placenta. Normally, shortly after the birth, a drug called syntometrine is given via an injection in the thigh to make the womb contract so that the placenta comes out quickly. It can also help to prevent heavy bleeding and haemorrhaging and the placenta is usually expelled within five minutes of birth. However, if you prefer, you can wait for the placenta to come out naturally. This usually takes up to half an hour. If you've been given syntometrine,

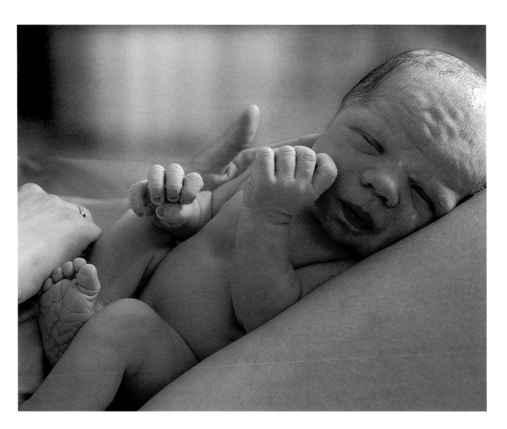

your midwife will pull gently on the cord to encourage the placenta to come out and will check that it is intact and complete.

Once the placenta has been delivered, you will be cleaned up. Meanwhile, your baby will be weighed and measured. With your permission, your baby will be given a dose of vitamin K, which helps to prevent a rare bleeding disorder that affects some babies. If you want to spend some time alone with your partner and your new baby, this should be fine providing the delivery has gone well.

The Apgar test About a minute after the birth, your baby's general condition is checked by the midwife. She will assess her breathing, heart rate, colour, tone and responses, giving each a score of 0, 1 or 2. A total score of 7 or more means your baby is fine. The test is repeated after five minutes and it's not unusual for a baby to have a low first score which rises to 9 or 10 in the second test. If your baby has a very low score on her first test, she may need resuscitation. The Apgar test is intended to be a guide to your baby's well-being; if she scores a 10, it doesn't mean you've got a genius on your hands!

Postnatal **checks**

Special labours

Not every labour progresses quite in text-book fashion. If your baby needs extra help being born, your care team can choose from several special approaches to ensure she arrives safely

EVERYONE HOPES for a straightforward labour – and most women have one. However, some babies need extra help to be born vaginally, while others can only be delivered safely by caesarean section.

Assisted delivery

Sometimes, during the second stage of labour, the baby fails to move down from the womb to the vaginal opening. This may be because the mother's exhausted and can't push, or the baby's unexpectedly large or in a difficult position. If the baby is becoming short of oxygen, the medical team might use forceps or ventouse to help her out quickly in what is known as an assisted delivery. An assisted delivery can also become necessary if you've been given an epidural and you feel too numb to push in time with the contractions, or your blood pressure is high.

Forceps These look like a large pair of salad tongs and are fitted around the baby's head to ease her out in time with contractions (see right). If forceps are used, you'll be given a local anaesthetic in your pelvic floor area (if you haven't had an epidural)

and an episiotomy (see page 70). Sometimes the baby's head appears to be a bit bruised afterwards, but this soon heals. Forceps are currently used in about one in ten deliveries.

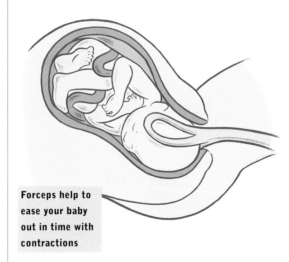

Forceps help to ease your baby out in time with contractions

Ventouse This looks a bit like a sink plunger and is a gentler alternative to forceps. A small cap is applied to the baby's head and the other end is attached to a suction pump (see above right). The vacuum that this creates sticks the cap to the top of the baby's head and allows the doctor to pull on it to ease the baby out.

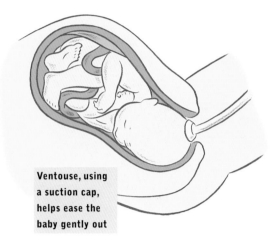

Ventouse, using
a suction cap,
helps ease the
baby gently out

Backache labour

In most deliveries, the baby's head faces the mother's spine. But in a posterior delivery, the baby's head faces the mother's stomach, with the back of the head pressing on her spine. In this case, contractions are felt as backache, often with shooting pains down the legs. Early on, getting on all fours and rocking your pelvis may relieve the pain and help turn the baby but, if labour is long, you may be advised to have an epidural.

Around half of all babies who are in a posterior position rotate during labour. A further 20 per cent require an assisted delivery and five per cent are born by caesarean.

Breech baby

Most babies settle into the cephalic position (head down), ready for birth, during the last couple of months of pregnancy. However, about three per cent of babies stay in a breech position (bottom down).

If your baby is in a breech position (see below) you may be able to feel her head pressing against your ribs.

Some obstetricians will try to turn a breech baby at about 38 weeks, while complementary therapies, such as yoga or acupuncture, may also be used to try to get the baby to turn. However, if your baby is still breech at the time of delivery, you will need special attention as a breech birth is more likely to produce complications.

Depending on your baby's exact position, it may be possible to have a vaginal delivery. Your obstetrician may do a scan to see if the baby is in a suitable position to try; if the baby isn't in a suitable position, you may be advised to have a caesarean (see page 74). If you do have a vaginal delivery, you'll probably be given an episiotomy.

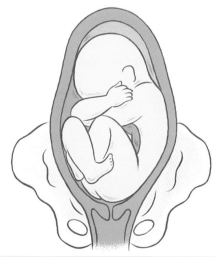

A baby in a breech position (bottom down) may
turn herself before labour begins

Caesarean

A caesarean section is an operation to take the baby out of the womb when it is not possible or safe to deliver the baby vaginally. The operation may be performed before labour begins or once it's underway.

● An elective caesarean is performed before labour begins – the baby may be in an awkward breech position, or it may be a multiple birth with the babies in a difficult position, or the mother may have a very small pelvis and a large baby. A woman may have a medical condition or a psychological reason why a vaginal delivery is not advisable and an elective caesarean preferable.

● An emergency caesarean is normally performed where labour has started but a problem has developed. This could include: the labour not progressing, the baby becoming distressed, the mother's pelvis appearing to be too small for the baby's head to pass through safely, or a problem with the placenta.

What happens A caesarean can be performed under a general anaesthetic (which means you'll be put to sleep) or an epidural. The advantages of an epidural are that your partner can stay with you and your baby can be delivered into your arms.

An epidural does not carry the risks that are associated with a general anaesthetic. But, some women prefer to have a general anaesthetic and, in an emergency, this may be the only option available to you.

Once the anaesthetic has taken effect, a cut about 15cm (6in) long is made just along the top of the pubic hair and the baby is lifted out, followed by the placenta. If this is done under an epidural, a screen will be put up to prevent you from seeing what's

Having a caesarean with an epidural means that you will normally be able to hold your baby straight away

happening, but your baby will be brought to you as soon as she is breathing well. She will usually be able to stay with you while the cut is stitched closed.

After a caesarean Recovery after a caesarean is slower than after a vaginal delivery. You will have to stay in hospital for longer (on average for about five days) and will be given painkillers while your abdomen heals. You can still breast-feed your baby, but you may need to experiment with different positions to find one that is comfortable (using pillows to cushion the wound can help).

You will also need more help at home as even lifting your baby can be painful for a couple of weeks. Partners, friends and relatives should understand this rather than

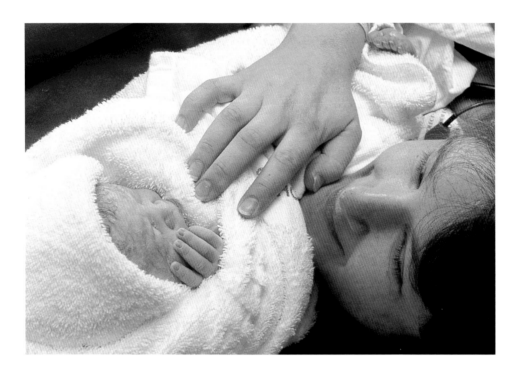

seeing a caesarean as an easy option, which it isn't. It's a major operation. If you know you will be going home to no support at all, you should tell your midwife.

Induction

Induction means starting labour artificially. There are a number of reasons why a pregnant woman may be induced: she may be past her due date which means the placenta may not be as efficient, she may have developed pre-eclampsia, which only disappears after the baby is born, or her baby may not be thriving in the womb. Induction may also be necessary when labour starts spontaneously but then stops, when the cervix isn't dilating, or when the waters break but contractions don't start. Methods include:

● Breaking the waters (ARM): the bag of amniotic fluid that surrounds the baby is punctured by inserting a small hook through the cervix. This can help to stimulate contractions.

● Gel or a pessary: these contain prostaglandin hormones which soften the cervix and encourage contractions. The gel or pessary is inserted into the vagina.

● Syntocinon drip: this contains the contraction-inducing substance, oxytocin. It's very effective, but makes contractions start powerfully and, as a result, most women need medical pain relief.

After the birth

The months of waiting are over and your baby is finally here. If your joy at meeting her is tempered by exhaustion, it's hardly surprising, given the changes that your body has been through

FOR MANY WOMEN, holding their newborn baby in their arms seems to erase the pain of labour instantly. But other women find that they are so exhausted they just want someone else to take care of the baby until they recover. Relief, joy, exhaustion and numbness are all natural reactions and during the next few days your emotions will be in flux. Try to take one day at a time.

Meeting your new baby

Your baby may look rather different to how you imagined she would. During delivery, her head will have been compressed and may be a slightly odd shape, especially if you have had an assisted delivery (see page 72). On top of her head you will notice a soft spot, called the fontanelle, where the skull bones haven't yet fused. She may still be coated in white vernix or have traces of downy hair (lanugo), and her genitals may seem large and out of proportion.

Some newborn babies appear to squint and while all black and Asian babies have brown eyes, for the first few weeks all white babies have blue eyes – they won't develop their final eye colour for about a month.

Bonding with your baby Only a generation ago, babies were routinely whisked away from their mothers at birth and taken to the nursery, to be returned only for feeding. Nowadays, however, your baby is more likely to be delivered into your arms and then stay with you most of the day and night.

Recent studies show that this immediate close contact is important in helping mothers to forge a strong link, or bond, with their babies. But some mothers worry that because they don't feel a rush of love and tenderness every time they look at or hold their baby, something has gone wrong and they will never bond with their baby. But this simply isn't true.

For many women, it takes several weeks of caring for their baby for that special bond to form. Falling in love with your baby from the moment you take her in your arms does not make you a better mother than the mother who only feels at ease with her baby after a few weeks. What matters most is that you continue to look after your baby. In time, the way she looks at you, and the way she curls her fingers

around yours and responds to you once she recognises your voice and touch, will gradually win you over.

The postnatal ward

Once you and your baby have recovered sufficiently from the birth, you will normally be sent to the postnatal ward. Here, midwives will show you how to care for your baby and help you establish breast-feeding. It can take time to get the hang of it, particularly with a first baby, so ask for any help you need. If you have had an epidural or a caesarean, you will be confined to bed for longer but your midwife will encourage you to get up and about as soon as possible.

Try and get as much rest as possible now – lots of women say they are too excited to sleep after the drama of labour and the arrival of their baby, but try to sleep when your baby does. Some babies sleep a lot immediately after the birth; others barely at all. If you have one of the second kind and are exhausted, ask the staff to take your baby for a couple of hours to give you a break.

Going home

Before you are discharged, a paediatrician will examine your baby to make sure she's healthy and ready to go home. Checks include assessing the baby visually, feeling the roof of the mouth to make sure it's complete, listening to heart and lungs, and checking your baby's organs. The feet, legs and spine will be looked at and the hips rotated to see that they're not dislocated. If your baby's a boy, his testicles will be checked to make sure they've descended.

Your body after birth

It takes time for your body to recover from giving birth. If you are in pain, speak to your midwife, who will be able to give you a painkiller. Remind them if you are breast-feeding, so that they can choose a painkiller that's suitable.

Bleeding You should expect fairly heavy bleeding, known as lochia, for the first few days after the birth. This is caused by bleeding from the site of the placenta and will become lighter and pinker by the end of the first week and should have stopped by the sixth. It's normal to have small clots in the blood, but if you have a large clot or the bleeding is very heavy, for example, you need more than one maternity towel an hour, tell hospital staff.

Uterine contractions You may find that you continue to experience contractions, similar to those you felt in labour, for several days after the birth as your womb contracts. This is more likely if you are breast-feeding, since breast-feeding encourages the womb to return to its normal size more quickly. If the contractions are extremely uncomfortable, tell your midwife who will be able to give you a painkiller, such as paracetamol.

The baby blues

Around three to five days after their baby is born, lots of women go through a short period of unhappiness, called 'the baby blues'. Symptoms of the baby blues include feeling weepy and easily upset, and they are caused by a combination of fluctuating hormones, tiredness and the emotional adjustments you are having to make. For most women the baby blues disappear within a few days.

Stitches If you have had an episiotomy, you may feel very sore and tender down below. Going to the toilet may be very painful and even sitting down can be uncomfortable. In the first few days after the birth, hospital staff may give you a painkiller to help ease the pain.

Sitting on a pillow, ice pack or a bag of frozen vegetables with a cloth wrapped around can also help. When you go to the toilet, dab gently with toilet paper, always wipe from front to back to avoid infection and keep the area clean. Try to avoid constipation and take care not to strain.

Your stitches don't need to be taken out and should eventually dissolve naturally after about five or six days. However, you should let the hospital staff know if your stitches feel as if they are pulling or if they feel like they're tightening, as very occasionally they need to be redone.

If you're in pain after giving birth, talk to your midwife who will be able to give you a painkiller

Bruising Even if you don't have stitches, you may still have considerable bruising around the vagina and the entire area may feel tender, sore and uncomfortable for a few days after giving birth.

Your breasts In the first few days after you give birth, your breasts will produce colostrum, a sort of pre-milk which is full of nourishment. Around day three or four, your milk will come in and your breasts may feel hot, hard, swollen and tender. This is called engorgement. If you plan to breast-feed, the best way to relieve this is by feeding your baby (she may need extra help with latching on when your breasts are engorged). Putting hot flannels on your breasts and taking warm baths may also help.

If you don't plan to breast-feed, wearing a supportive bra will help ease the discomfort, which will gradually subside as your milk eventually starts to dry up.

Your figure You may be surprised that giving birth doesn't mean regaining your pre-pregnancy figure immediately. You might have lost the combined weight of your baby, the placenta and the amniotic fluid, but the fat your body has laid down for breast-feeding, coupled with stretched tummy muscles, mean you may still look several months pregnant. It is possible to regain your figure, but your body has done something quite extraordinary in producing a baby and it will take time for your muscles to regain tone.

Now is not the time to start dieting or running around the wards. To be realistic, you should expect it to take at least a year for your body to recover completely. But, there are some exercises you can start right away, including pelvic floor exercises (see page 18) and the ones featured in the box below. Your obstetric physiotherapist may also give you exercises to do at home.

Gentle exercises

Exercise your lungs
Lie on your back with your knees bent and feet flat on the floor. Place your hands on your stomach and breathe in, feeling your stomach expand, then breathe out completely, pulling the stomach muscles in towards your back to squeeze out as much air as possible. Repeat this exercise several times – it improves circulation, strengthens abdominal muscles and helps you to relax.

Improve your circulation
Still lying on your back, flatten your knees and flex your ankles, then circle each ankle in both directions. This helps to improve your circulation. Do this exercise several times a day.

Stretch your spine
Stand with your heels a few inches away from a wall, then lean back against it. Press your waist back so you can feel your whole spine touching the wall. Pull your stomach muscles in. Stretch yourself up tall, then relax. Try to walk tall whenever you are walking so you can start to realign your posture.

Your special care baby

If your new baby needs extra care when she arrives, a special care unit with its sophisticated equipment and highly trained staff will give her the very best chance of getting fit and well

THE SPECIAL CARE BABY UNIT (SCBU) or neonatal intensive care unit of a hospital is where babies who need specialist care are looked after. Sometimes, if a baby is very ill, she may be transferred to a regional centre where there are facilities for intensive nursing. However, the majority of babies are looked after at local units.

Who needs special care?

Around one in ten babies will spend time in a SCBU – most will spend only two or three days there, although a few may stay longer. There may be several reasons why:

Multiple births Twins and triplets are often born early – twins are generally born around 37 weeks and triplets around week 33. As they're more likely to be premature or small, around 40 per cent of multiple birth babies spend some time in special care.

Premature birth A baby is considered premature if she is born before the 37th week of pregnancy. If your baby is born prematurely, try not to worry about her appearance. She will be fully formed but will be smaller, thinner and redder than full-term babies. Her head may seem large and

Around one in ten babies will spend some time in a special care unit – most of them only two or three days

Breathing problems Babies who are very small when they're born may have breathing and circulation difficulties, which means that they'll need to spend some time in a special care baby unit. The unit will be fitted with equipment that can help tiny babies with their breathing and circulation and, if they need it, feeding (see page 83).

her movements abrupt. However, as she gets stronger, she'll start to fill out. Babies born before the 24th week of pregnancy have only a slim chance of survival as their lungs aren't fully formed. After this date, their chances improve week by week and some babies who are born after the 34th week do not need any kind of special care.

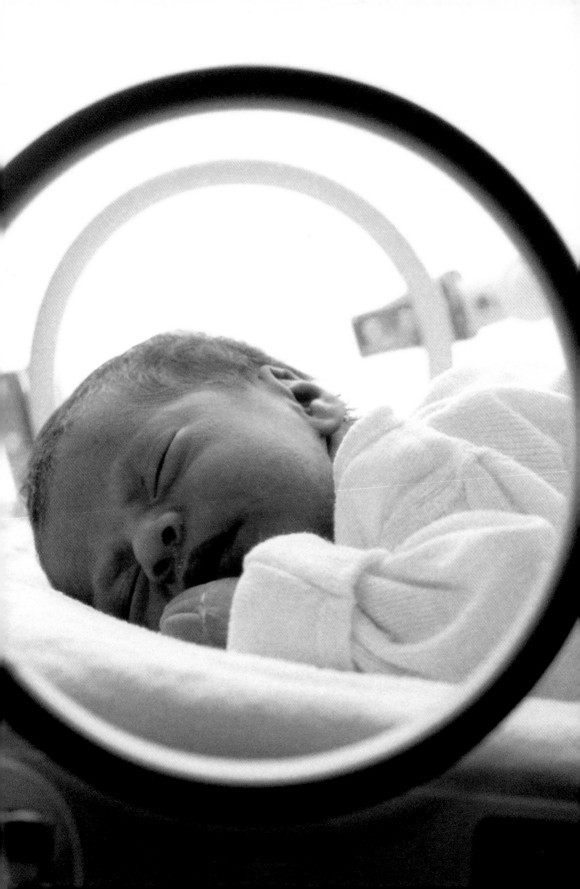

Jaundice Babies are born with a surplus of red blood cells which are broken down after they are born. This creates a yellowish substance called bilirubin, usually excreted via the liver. If a baby's liver can't cope, bilirubin builds up in the blood, making the skin and whites of the eyes yellow.

Many babies have mild jaundice which clears up on its own, but some babies need phototherapy (a kind of light therapy) to break down the bilirubin. If your baby needs phototherapy, an eye shield will be put over her eyes and she will be placed under a special light. This might be done on the postnatal ward, but if jaundice is severe, special care may be needed. Jaundice usually disappears after a week.

Medical problems Some babies go into the special care unit because they have major medical difficulties, such as a heart defect, or they may be there to recover from major surgery.

The special care unit

Babies in a special care unit are looked after by a team of highly-specialised doctors and nurses. In the unit, there may be a section for intensive care and another for babies needing less help, but there will always be a much higher ratio of medical staff to babies than on an ordinary ward.

To almost all parents, the amount of medical equipment in the ward will seem intimidating at first. However, knowing what each piece of equipment is for can help you feel less daunted (see box, right). You should also feel free to ask any questions about your baby's care, condition and the tangle of tubes and equipment that surrounds her.

Your role It is natural to be anxious if your baby is in a special care baby unit. However, you can play a vital role in your baby's recovery. Staff welcome parents to the special care unit because research shows that babies who are held, stroked, cuddled and talked to by their parents do better than those who are not.

If your baby's condition permits, it's a good idea to get involved in simple baby care tasks such as changing nappies or, as your baby gets stronger, giving her a bath. If your baby has a feeding tube, staff will show you how to express your breast milk so that it can be fed to her via the tube. If your baby was born prematurely, she will derive particular benefit from receiving your breast milk.

An incubator is a covered perspex cot which helps to keep your baby warm and maintains the correct temperature around her. There is normally a hole shaped like a porthole at the side which allows you to reach in and stroke or hold your baby.

A ventilator is used, for instance, if your baby's lungs are not developed enough to allow her to breathe for herself. It takes over the breathing function for her and works like a pump, passing air through a tube in your baby's mouth and into her windpipe. The air is moistened and warmed by a humidifier to prevent your baby's lungs from drying out. Once your baby's lungs are mature, she will be taken off the ventilator and allowed to breathe for herself.

Monitors are often used to check on babies in special care units to ensure that everything is as it should be. The sound of monitors and bleeps can be alarming to a parent, but they are there to let staff know when your baby requires attention. Remember, the units are staffed by highly-trained nurses who know exactly how to respond. The monitors include:
* A saturation monitor and gas analyzer which measure oxygen and carbon dioxide in your baby's blood
* An ECG to measure heart rate and rhythm
* A temperature monitor fixed to your baby's skin to check her temperature stays within the correct range. Premature babies in particular are not very good at controlling their own temperature
* A blood pressure machine to monitor changes in your baby's circulation.

An apnoea alarm is a small pad that monitors babies who are breathing for themselves, but who may occasionally forget to do so. The pad is placed under the baby and sounds an alarm if she stops making breathing movements.

A drip supplies your baby with food directly into her blood-stream, or she may have a feeding tube that runs through her nose into her throat. Some babies are well enough not to need a tube and can be breast-fed or fed with a cup or bottle.

Getting through it Having a baby in special care is a difficult time. You expected to leave hospital with your baby. Instead, you may have been discharged while your baby is left in special care. This can leave you feeling very low. However, remember that most babies make a complete recovery and that, while this time is difficult, it will soon fade into insignificance once your baby is home. Your baby will normally be discharged when she can breathe and feed well and is considered a healthy weight.

Alternatively, if your baby is expected to be in special care for weeks rather than a day or two, or is very unwell, you may find yourself on a roller coaster of hope and despair, your mood swinging with each development. All you can do is take it one day at a time and get as much support and rest as you can. The organisation BLISS has a helpline for parents of premature babies and you may find it helpful to talk to someone who really understands what you are going through (see page 168).

Caring for your baby

This chapter covers most of
the practical baby care
tasks you'll face in the first
year, from changing a
nappy to introducing your
baby to real food

Buying baby equipment

Modern baby equipment makes the business of caring for your baby easier than it's ever been. Items that you use every day will come in for lots of wear and tear, so buy the best you can

HAVING A BABY can be expensive, but knowing what's essential and what's not, in terms of equipment, will help keep costs under control. When you are buying major items, explore all the options carefully and think about what you really need before you buy. It's also worth keeping all receipts just in case, for example, the car seat doesn't fit your car or you change your mind about the type of pram you want.

Getting around

Prams and pushchairs The type of pram or pushchair you choose will depend on your lifestyle. If you get around mainly on foot, but rarely use public transport, you will probably be better off choosing a pram-combination, which is the modern equivalent of the traditional carriage pram. Pram-combinations may consist of a carry-cot-pram which can be turned into a pushchair, or a chassis that holds a separate carrycot, pushchair and even a car seat. If you use public transport, a sling and lightweight pushchair suitable from birth may be a better investment.

Consider the following before you buy:
- Is it easy to fold and unfold?
- Can you lift it if necessary?
- Is the height of the handle adjustable?
- Are the assembly instructions clear?
- Are the brakes efficient and easy to use?
- Is there a well-fitted five-point harness?

Car seat If you own a car, a baby car seat is essential from the moment you leave the hospital with your baby. It's important to check the car seat is fitted correctly before every journey. Once your baby is in his car seat, adjust the harness so that only two fingers can be inserted between the harness and your baby. Never put a car seat in the front if the passenger side has an airbag.

Choose between transportable car seats and ones that are fixed in the car – but always look out for the safety standard ECE R44.03. Transportable seats can be used indoors as a seat for your baby and, if your baby has fallen asleep, they allow you to take him indoors without waking him up. Some are suitable for babies weighing up to 13kg (29lb). Seats that stay in the car can be used until your child is 18kg (40lb).

Other travel items

- Sling – newborn babies love them. It's a great way to carry your baby and keep your hands free, too. Try it on in the shop to see how easy it is to put on and take off.
- Insect net/cat net.
- Rain-cover, canopy or parasol, and foot-muff for the pushchair.

Feeding

If you plan to breast-feed, you'll only need to buy equipment for when you express milk. But, if you plan to bottle-feed, you will need a range of feeding equipment (see page 110) right from day one.

Nursery essentials

- Cradle, Moses basket, carrycot or cot (Many parents put their newborn baby in a cradle or basket to sleep, then move him into a cot when he is a little older.)
- At least three fitted and three flat sheets, and at least three blankets
- Mattress (BS 1877: Part 10) that fits properly – there should be no room for your baby's hand to get trapped between the mattress and the side. Those with a fitted waterproof layer are a good buy.
- Thermometer to check room temperature
- Baby monitor (This is only essential if your baby is likely to be out of earshot for any length of time.)

Changing and bathing essentials

- Changing mat
- Cotton wool (This is recommended for cleaning newborn babies' bottoms as it doesn't dry the skin. Later, many parents prefer the convenience of baby wipes.)
- Disposable or recyclable nappies (see page 92) – bear in mind that a baby can get through up to ten a day at first.
- Nappy bin and nappy bags
- Changing bag for transporting nappies and cleaning kit when you are out
- Baby shampoo and soft baby brush
- Soft towel or a baby changing robe
- Safety support or foam mat, to help prevent your baby slipping in the bath
- Baby nail clippers/scissors
- Muslin squares – to keep you clean!

Clothing essentials

- Six bodysuits (these have poppers at the crotch to prevent them riding up) or vests
- Six sleepsuits
- Two lightweight cardigans or jumpers
- Two pairs of booties
- A sun hat for summer
- A 'snow suit' or coat, two warm hats and one pair of mittens for winter.

The first weeks

No matter how much you've longed for your baby's arrival, nothing can quite prepare you for your first weeks as a mother and the enormous changes your baby will bring to your life

EVERYONE'S EXPERIENCES in the first couple of weeks after the birth are different. Much depends on how easy or difficult the birth was, and on how much your baby sleeps and feeds. Many newborn babies feed every two hours or less, and without a pattern, so for the first few weeks there will be very little routine in your life. Don't expect too much of yourself – for now, it's best just to go with the flow.

Time to recover

Labour is exhausting and you need to recover, so it's important not to take on too much – don't accept visitors around the clock, spring-clean or phone in to work at the first opportunity.

Bear in mind that some babies are very sleepy at first but suddenly become more active – particularly at night. If you have a baby who sleeps a lot to begin with, take every opportunity to rest while you can.

Don't plan too many big outings, but do try to get out once a day. Tiny babies can be at their most demanding in the evening – this is a good time to hand over to someone else and have a bath or a nap, if you can.

How will you feel?

During these first few weeks you may feel as if your life has been turned upside down. You may be thrilled with your new baby one day and then wish you could send him back the next. You may feel almost normal in the morning and then be willing to sell your house for a few hours' sleep by the small hours. Although these early weeks can be tough, they do pass. As your baby grows and needs to feed less often, and sleeps for longer stretches, life will gradually begin to get easier. It helps if you and your partner can support each other and talk through your feelings.

A midwife will call on you regularly for up to ten days once you get home, or longer if you or your baby need extra care. She'll check that your womb is contracting and any stitches are healing, and that feeding is progressing well. She'll answer any questions you may have, too. **After ten days**, a health visitor will normally take over. She's a specially trained nurse who can offer advice and support on baby care and family problems until your child is five years old.

Postnatal care

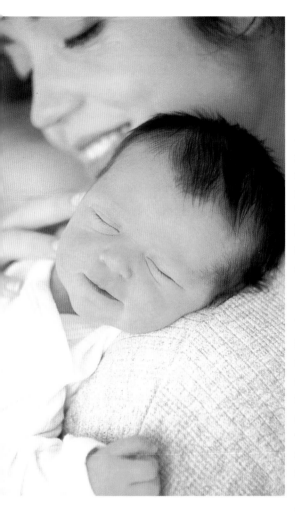

Becoming a parent is a major life change and you are bound to experience a mixture of emotions. Elation, excitement, worry, tenderness, tiredness, frustration and feeling generally fed up are just a few of them. On the third or fourth day after your baby is born, you may also experience 'the baby blues', which are caused by a combination of hormonal changes, tiredness and emotional factors, which together will make you feel weepy and vulnerable. This should soon pass, but if you continue to feel like this for more than a few days, talk to your health visitor or doctor about it.

Although most people concentrate on the mother's needs at this time, fathers are also undergoing a huge life change and they too may be beset with worries and uncertainty. Try to involve your partner in caring for his baby and be careful not to criticise his efforts – don't forget, you've probably already had much more practice than him.

Dealing with visitors

With a new baby in the house, you may find yourself suddenly swamped with visitors. Some parents love entertaining and enjoy the attention. Others find a constant stream of people just adds to their weariness and confusion. However you feel, keep visitors at a manageable level and give them a definite time to visit, so that they don't take away all your opportunities to rest.

The ideal visitor is one who is reassuring and sympathetic, and takes your baby for a few minutes to allow you to get dressed, grab a quick snack or take a bath. However, if you find that your visitors are not like this, don't feel you have to run around after them or rush about tidying up before they arrive. This is the one time when your visitors should look after you.

Sometimes close family members are not sure what they should or shouldn't be doing to lend a hand. It's useful if you can be open about what kind of support you need at this time – whether it's help with the weekly shop or someone to take over nappy-changing duty temporarily.

Baby care basics

There's no single way to change your baby's nappy or give him a bath – but there's usually an easy way. Once you've mastered the basic techniques, you can adapt them to suit you and your baby

AT FIRST, EVEN PICKING UP your baby can seem a complicated manoeuvre, let alone changing, dressing or bathing him. But, with practice, these skills will quickly become second nature.

Lifting and holding

The most important thing to remember whenever you lift or hold your baby is to support his head and neck until his muscles are sufficiently developed (at around four or five months) for him to do it himself.

To pick your baby up when he is lying on his back, lean over him to get your body close to his. Slide one hand under his bottom and the other under his neck and head from the opposite direction. This will have the effect of forming a cradle with your arms. Lift your baby firmly towards you. When you put him back down, support his head and neck with one arm and lower his body with the other. When he's safely back on a level surface, carefully slide your arms out.

You'll quickly discover how your baby likes to be held and what suits you best, but here are some ideas for the early days:

● Cradle hold: Once you've picked your baby up, you can simply hold him against your chest, with his head and neck supported in the crook of your elbow.

● Shoulder hold: You can hold your baby against your shoulder so that he is upright, with his head resting either on or below your shoulder. Support his head with your hand. When your baby is older and can support his own head, he will enjoy this position as it allows him to look around.

● Tummy soother (see illustration below): This is good if your baby has wind, as the pressure of your hand on his tummy will be soothing. Pick your baby up, turn him over carefully (still supporting his head and neck) and lay him face-down along one arm, with his head facing your elbow. Use this arm to hold him against you. Slide your free hand under his tummy with the palm facing upwards.

Dressing your baby

What should he wear? For the first month, your baby will probably need to wear one layer of clothing more than you. A vest, a sleepsuit and, if necessary, a cardigan is fine for indoors. If you're taking him outside in the cold, put a hat on him as well as his outdoor suit – babies lose heat quickly from their head. A sun hat is useful for the summer (but keep small babies in the shade). If it's hot and your baby isn't wearing much, apply a sun-screen suitable for babies (factor 20+).

Putting on a vest Lay your baby on his back on his changing mat. Take the vest and, holding it with the front of the neck edge towards you, gather all the material.

• Put the back edge behind the top of your baby's head, then gently pull the gathered material over his head.

• Gather one sleeve and ease your baby's arm through, then repeat with the other sleeve. Make sure you pull the material and not your baby. Pull the vest down and do up the poppers, if there are any.

Putting on a sleepsuit Undo all the poppers and lay the sleepsuit out on the changing mat. Lie your baby on top so his neck lines up with the neck of the suit.

• Gather up the material in one leg and slip your baby's toes into the foot of the sleepsuit. Ease the material over his leg. Do the same with the other leg.

• Gather up the material in one of the sleeves and slip it over your baby's hand. Hold his hand between your thumb and fingers as you ease the material up his arm. Remember to pull the material, not his hand. Repeat with the other sleeve. Fasten the poppers, starting at the bottom and working upwards.

• To undress him, reverse the manoeuvre, supporting his head as you lift him.

All about nappies

Most new mothers use disposable nappies for convenience, but recyclables are becoming more popular due to environmental concerns. New designs which use velcro rather than safety pins for fastening and which don't require complex folding make today's recyclables more attractive than traditional terry nappies. In some areas, there are laundering services which deliver a bag of cotton nappies to your door, complete with nappy bin, and remove the dirty nappies for laundering later in the week. For details about non-disposable nappy services in your area, contact the Real Nappy Association (see page 169).

What's in a nappy? The contents of your baby's nappies will change over the first few weeks. How they end up will depend on how he is fed. If he's breast-fed, he will have yellowy-orange stools that are quite watery (often bits of milk curd are visible). If he's bottle-fed, his stools will be firmer, pale brown and more smelly. Don't worry if he goes red and cries as he dirties his nappy – this is normal. If your baby's stools suddenly become pale or creamy (especially if he has had jaundice or his skin has a yellow tinge), talk to your doctor. If his stools change otherwise, but he seems fine, talk to your midwife or health visitor.

In the early weeks, your baby will need changing often, perhaps every two hours. His digestive system has a lot to get used to

and he may produce a number of dirty nappies a day. As he settles into a feeding routine, his nappies will need changing less often – although it's still important to change him regularly to keep him feeling comfortable and prevent nappy rash.

Changing your baby

Before you start changing your baby's nappy, get everything to hand: a clean nappy, cotton wool and a bowl of warm water, and tissues for drying (or wipes, once your baby's a month old).

● Lay your baby on a changing mat, with a towel underneath him in case of accidents. Undo the nappy – if you have a boy, wait a

moment – baby boys love to wee the minute they feel fresh air! If the nappy's dirty, wipe away most of the faeces with a clean part of the nappy. Fold the nappy down under your baby's bottom.

● Clean the nappy area using moistened cotton wool. Lift your baby gently by his legs, holding his ankles in one hand with a finger in-between. For a girl, wipe from front to back to avoid getting germs into the vagina. For a boy, carefully clean the foreskin but don't pull it back. Put the dirty cotton wool inside the nappy and set aside.

● Dry your baby's bottom with tissues. Help keep his skin healthy by allowing him to kick on his changing mat for a couple of minutes without a nappy on.

● Protect your baby's skin with a barrier cream if he is sore, then unfold the new nappy. Place it beneath your baby so the tabs are at the back, level with his waist, and the pattern is at the front. Fold the nappy up over your baby's tummy, hold flat and stick the tabs across.

● Move your baby to a safe place while you bag and bin the nappy and wash your hands thoroughly. If you are using non-disposable nappies, you'll need a nappy bucket and sanitising solution. If the nappy is dirty, flush the contents down the loo and rinse the nappy in the flushing water. Then soak it in a bucket filled with water and sanitising solution, and put it in the washing machine on a hot wash. Don't use a biological washing powder – it can irritate your baby's skin.

Keeping your baby clean

When your baby gets older, bath time can become a fun-packed part of the daily routine for both of you. However, when you first bring your baby home, you're unlikely to feel like bathing him every day and may not feel very confident about handling him. If you don't want to give your baby a daily bath, topping and tailing is a simple way of getting all his really important bits clean.

Topping and tailing Gather together everything you need: a small bowl of warm water and cotton wool for cleaning his face; a larger bowl of warm water and a flannel for cleaning the rest of his body; and a soft towel for drying him afterwards.

● Make sure the room is warm. Undress your baby and lay him on his changing mat.
● Use the flannel to wipe his mouth, chin and neck, paying special attention to the folds of his neck. Moisten a piece of cotton wool with water from the small bowl and wipe around his nostrils (not in them). Then use a fresh piece of cotton wool to wipe behind (not inside) his ears. Dry him gently.
● Use a fresh piece of moistened cotton wool to wipe from the inner corner of one eye outwards. Repeat for the other eye, using a new, clean piece of cotton wool.
● Use the flannel and water from the larger bowl to wash his hands and under his arms. Dry him gently.
● Wash his nappy area thoroughly, then dry him and put on a clean nappy.

Bathing a new baby At first, you'll probably find it easier to bath your baby in a baby bath or sink, rather than a big bath. If you find holding a slippery baby tricky, buy a special support or foam mat to make it easier – but never leave him alone, even for a few seconds. To make bathing easier:
● Get together all your baby's bathing things, including a soft towel, a clean nappy, changing kit and clean clothes.
● Make sure the bathroom is warm. Run cold water into the baby bath, then add hot water (not the other way around). Test the

If you don't want to give your baby a daily bath, topping and tailing is a good way of getting him clean

temperature of the bath water with your elbow – it should be pleasantly warm, not hot. Don't use your hand to test bath temperatures – what feels tepid to your hand could burn your baby. You can also buy simple thermometers with heat indicator strips which are designed for testing bath water. Cover the taps with flannels if they are close to the baby bath or if you are bathing your baby in the sink.

● Undress your baby and clean his bottom if necessary. Settle him in the crook of your elbow, with your arm around his back and your thumb and fingers encircling the top of his outside arm. Use your free hand to lift and lower him by his bottom into the bath. Keep hold of his arm while he is in the bath and use your free hand to splash water gently' over him. You can use cotton wool to clean his face.

● When your baby has had enough, slide your free hand under his bottom and lift him out, making sure his neck and head are well supported. Wrap him in his towel and dry him off carefully, paying attention to all of his creases. Finally, put on a clean nappy and dress him.

Washing your baby's hair Hair can be washed about once a week as part of your baby's bath time routine. The easiest way to do it is to hold your baby in the bath and wet his hair with a dribble of water from a flannel or sponge. Pour a little baby shampoo onto his head, then with your free hand, gently rub his head. Be careful not to press on his fontanelle (the soft spot on top). Use the sponge to rinse the suds off. When your baby is able to sit up in the bath, you can use a head guard to protect his face from bubbles during hair washes if they trouble him.

Bathing an older baby Once your baby can sit on his own, you can move him into the big bath. To make the transition easier, try putting his baby bath in the big bath for a few days first. Once he's in the big bath, a rubber mat will prevent him from slipping over as he makes a grab for his bath-time toys. Sponges for squeezing, pots for pouring and bottles for squirting will all help him to make fascinating discoveries about water. But, however safe and happy he looks, never leave him alone in the bath. It only takes seconds for a baby to drown.

Crying and comforting

Your baby's cry is hard to ignore – and with reason. It's designed by nature to provoke a response from you. The quicker you can work out what your baby needs, the sooner his crying will stop

UNTIL THEY BEGIN TO SMILE at about six weeks, crying is the only way babies have of expressing themselves. Some cry for easily understood reasons; others may cry almost non-stop and be difficult to comfort. Often babies are at their most irritable in the evening and this is when you can expect more prolonged crying.

Why your baby cries

As your baby gets used to the world around him, he'll gradually cry less and less. You'll also get better at understanding why he's crying and what you need to do to comfort him.

Hunger This is probably the number one cause of crying in a very young baby, especially if he hasn't had a feed for a couple of hours. Breast-fed babies, in particular, have no routine in the early days and are often hungry again soon after their last feed. Babies also go through phases, when they seem to be more hungry than usual. If hunger is the problem, giving your baby a feed should stop the crying instantly.

Wind Most newborn babies are affected by wind to some extent. It causes tummy pain and even makes some babies bring up their feed. Bottle-fed babies tend to swallow more wind when drinking their milk than breast-fed babies. Holding your baby in an upright position after his feed will give any wind that's present the chance to rise to the top of his stomach and escape as a burp.

There are different ways to 'wind' your baby – experiment to find what suits him best. Try sitting him on your lap and supporting his head with a hand under his chin, or holding him against your shoulder, rubbing and patting his back gently. Sometimes, rubbing a baby's stomach gently works, too. Babies with severe wind may be suffering from colic (see page 99). Once your baby can sit up, wind is unlikely to be a problem.

Needing comfort Babies often cry when they want to be close to a familiar person. After all, it was snug and warm in the womb; outside it can feel strange and lonely. You may find that carrying your

Illness Babies tend to cry more than usual when they're sick. Even if your baby only has a minor cold, this may prevent him from feeding or sucking in the way that he is used to and will make him feel distressed. If your baby is crying more than usual and his cry sounds different in some way, particularly if he has other symptoms of illness, consult your doctor.

A dirty nappy This will cause enough discomfort to make some babies cry, whereas others won't even notice when their nappy needs changing. If your baby has nappy rash, he will also cry more. The solution in this case is to change his nappy more often to help the nappy rash heal.

Wanting to sleep Some babies find it hard to settle, and cry miserably before they eventually drop off. Rocking your baby in your arms, dimming the lights and walking him up and down, or taking him for a walk in his pram are all ways of helping him to get to sleep. Baby swings and chairs can help, as many babies find the rhythmic motion very calming – try putting your baby in one after his evening bath to get him in the mood for sleep.

baby in a sling is an effective way to soothe him or that he is comforted by being swaddled tightly in a shawl. If your baby finds having his nappy changed or being undressed distressing, handle him gently but firmly and talk to him to reassure him – he'll soon grow out of this phase.

Lots of babies like to suck for comfort. If you are breast-feeding, you may find that, given the chance, your baby loves nothing more than to spend hours on end clamped to your breast. Or you may find that a dummy (or soother) works magic. If you don't want your baby to become hooked on his dummy, try to ease him off it at about three months old.

If your baby really won't settle, put him in his car seat and take him for a drive. You can also try buying tape recordings of womb music which can help to soothe your baby into sleep by recreating the sounds he heard before he was born.

When your baby is older

As your baby gets older, colic and wind become less of a problem, although he may still cry when he's hungry, wants a cuddle or has a dirty nappy. There will also be new reasons why your baby might cry.

Tiredness Babies often become tearful when they're tired, although – apart from the tears – they often do a very good job of hiding their tiredness. Once you get to know your baby, you'll begin to recognise how he behaves when he's tired. Until he's at least 12 months old, he's likely to need two naps a day and making sure that he gets them will help reduce this kind of crying.

Frustration As he becomes more aware of the world around him, your baby will want to explore things for himself. When his ambitions outstrip his abilities, he may express his frustration with tears and screaming – it's a natural part of growing up. All you can do is try and work out what it is that he is trying to do and help him to achieve it – it could be something as simple as trying to reach a cup of juice that is just beyond his grasp.

If your baby wants to do something he isn't allowed to, the best tactic is to divert his attention elsewhere as quickly as possible – give him a cuddle, talk to him or give him something interesting to play with.

When your baby's ambitions outstrip his abilities, he may express frustration with tears and screaming

Being trapped indoors on a wet day with a crying and inconsolable baby is enough to bring anyone to the end of their tether. But however angry and frustrated you feel, never shake your baby – this can cause brain damage, or even death. Instead:
• **Put** your baby in a safe place – his cot is ideal. Leave the room and go somewhere where his cries are less audible. Make a drink, sit and read or listen to music for a while. Only return to your baby when you feel calm enough to be sure you won't hurt him. He is safer in his cot than with an adult who is about to snap.
• **Call** a friend, relative or neighbour and ask them to come over to give you a break.

• **Phone** your health visitor or a helpline such as Serene (see page 169).
• **Seek** support from organisations like Home-Start. The National Childbirth Trust also has volunteers who can support new mums. If you have a baby with special needs, Contact A Family can put you in touch with others in a similar situation (see pages 168-169).
• **Don't** blame yourself. Having an 'off' day when you feel unable to cope does not make you a bad mother. However, if you continue to feel unable to cope or are angry with your baby, talk to your doctor as it's possible that you could be suffering from postnatal depression (see page 141).

When you want to cry

Separation anxiety From around the age of six to eight months, your baby may start to cry and get upset if he is separated from you – even if you've left the room for a few seconds and are only briefly out of sight. He'll grow out of this eventually, but in the meantime it can be difficult for you if you need a bit of time to yourself or if you have to leave him to go back to work. Reassurance and plenty of cuddles will help to comfort and calm him.

If your baby is looked after by a relative or trusted carer, chances are his tears will stop as soon as you step outside the door, particularly if he is distracted. However, if he seems highly reluctant and upset about going to a particular person, it may be that he is trying to tell you something.

Dealing with **colic**

Colic affects all babies to some degree but it is a particular problem in around one in five. Although 90 per cent of babies eventually grow out of colic at around three months, it causes misery for baby and parents while it lasts.

Colic often starts when babies are about a month old. It is characterised by bouts of uncontrollable crying with knees drawn up to the chest, a rigid back and face screwed up in misery. It's often worse at night when crying can last for hours.

The causes of colic are not clear, but the most common theory is that the baby's immature gut traps wind which becomes painful. There are many suggested solutions for it, but it's generally a case of trial and error to find out what works best for your baby. Common colic remedies include:

• Over-the-counter colic remedies from your pharmacist, such as Infacol
• Gripe water, which should only be given once your baby is one month old
• Sugar water, made by dissolving three teaspoons of sugar in a cup of cooled, boiled water. Give your baby half a teaspoon when colic strikes. If it doesn't work after several attempts, try something else.
• Very weak, cooled camomile tea
• Homeopathy and other complementary therapies. See a reputable practitioner
• Cranial osteopathy is sometimes used to relieve colic and it's becoming increasingly popular. The osteopath manipulates the baby's skull and skeleton, and attempts to relieve compression of the skull and other birth stresses which may be linked with colic. For more details, contact the Osteopathic Information Service who can supply you with a list of practitioners in your area (see page 169).

Sleep and your baby

Your new baby can't go more than a few hours without feeding, so disturbed nights are inevitable at the start. However, over the first year, his sleep pattern will slowly become more like yours

Y OUR NEWBORN BABY will sleep exactly when he wants and for as long as he needs. Unfortunately, this won't be at the times that you're used to sleeping. It will probably be some time before he learns to take all his sleep at night and to stay awake for the whole day.

The first six months

The average newborn baby sleeps for about 16 hours a day – although many new parents will find this hard to believe. While some babies sleep soundly for hours at a stretch right from the beginning and are 'going through the night' (sleeping for eight hours at a time) within a couple of months, the majority of newborn babies are not like this. Many sleep for a couple of hours at a time then wake for a feed, making no distinction between night and day. The most difficult are those who either sleep all day and stay awake all night, and those who only ever sleep for an hour or so at a time.

If your baby is under a month old, it is best to just go with the flow and rest whenever you can. You can, however, start encouraging him to recognise the difference between night and day by keeping the bedroom dark at night and making night feeds more businesslike (no playing). Most babies start to realise that night-time is for sleeping at around six to eight weeks, although they may still wake several times a night and have long naps in the day. Slowly, your baby will sleep for longer at night, with quite a few babies sleeping through the night from as early as three months.

> **Family beds**
>
> **When he's young**, you'll probably find it easier to get your baby to sleep when he's in bed with you rather than in his cot. Some experts believe that allowing your baby to share your bed is a good thing, while others are not so sure about the positive benefits. Many parents enjoy having their baby in bed with them, but the main drawback is that it is hard to persuade a baby who has got used to sharing his parents' bed to move into a cot.
> **One way** to compromise is to feed and settle your new baby in your bed and then move him into his own cradle or cot beside your bed once he's fallen asleep.
> **However**, if you or your partner have had alcohol, smoke or have taken drugs (including prescription medication), you shouldn't have your baby in your bed.

From six months

By the time your baby is six months old, he will probably be big enough not to need a feed during the night – although he is still likely to need a bedtime feed and an early morning feed. If your baby was premature, it may take him a little longer to sleep through the night.

Dropping night feeds If you have a six-month-old baby who is still waking several times a night, you can encourage him to stop waking by slowly reducing the amount of milk you give at night or gradually replacing it with cool, boiled water. This gives your baby less incentive to wake

up. If you are trying to stop night feeds, make sure your baby has plenty of milk during the day. If necessary, shorten the gap between daytime feeds.

Introducing a routine If you find it difficult to get your baby to sleep in the evening, it might help to establish a bedtime routine. Over time, your baby will realise that this routine means that bedtime is coming up and should settle more easily.

A typical routine might start half an hour after your baby's bedtime feed with a warm bath, followed by a story or song in your baby's room. Or you could try giving half the bedtime feed, followed by quiet play,

then the remainder of the feed, followed by teeth cleaning, a book and bed. When your baby is ready for bed, put him in his cot, kiss him goodnight, turn out the light and leave the room. Don't be too quick to go back to him if he starts crying. He may need a few minutes to settle on his own.

Sleep training If your baby is still waking frequently at night after almost a year, you may wish to try some sleep training. This involves leaving your baby to cry at night in his cot and, for it to work, you'll need to feel determined enough to stick out some noisy nights for at least a week.

Before you start, check that there's no reason why your baby is waking at night, particularly if it's a recent occurrence. Make sure that he is well and that he is safe in his cot. When your baby cries in the night, go to him, but don't pick him up. Instead, tell him gently, but firmly, that you love him but it's time to go to sleep. Leave the room even if he starts crying again. Stay away for a few minutes, then return and do exactly the same again. Repeat, lengthening the gaps between your return to up to ten minutes. Remember, provided your baby is safely in his cot, no harm will come to him.

Stick with this until your baby falls asleep – at first it might take three hours – but after several days the intervals between waking should increase as your baby realises there's no 'reward' to be had by waking.

Getting help If your baby's sleeping pattern is making your life a misery, many health centres now have sleep clinics which can offer advice. Ask your GP or health visitor for a referral. Alternatively, the support group Serene has tips for encouraging poor sleepers to sleep better (see page 169).

Cot death

Cot death is the sudden, unexplained death of a baby. Organisations like the Foundation for the Study of Infant Deaths (see page 168) are continuing to research the causes. Cot death is rare and there are ways to reduce the risk:

• **Always** put your baby on his back to sleep. Older babies can turn over – let them find their own sleeping position. Cot death after six months is extremely rare.

• **Make sure** his head stays uncovered. Put him to sleep with his feet at the foot of the cot and tuck in the blankets so they can't slip up and cover his head.

• **Stop** smoking when you're pregnant – even smoking ten cigarettes a day can increase the risk of cot death five-fold. The risk increases if your partner smokes as well, so ask him to stop, too. Make your home a smoke-free zone.

• **Don't** let your baby get too hot. Ideally, his bedroom should be 18°C (65°F) when he will need only a sheet and two blankets. It's normal for a baby's hands and feet to feel cool when he's asleep.

• **Remove** his outdoor clothes as soon as you come indoors or enter a warm car or bus, even if this means waking your baby.

• **Seek** medical advice if you're worried that your baby may be unwell.

Feeding your baby

Before your baby arrives, you need to think about how you would like to feed him. He will thrive on either breast or formula milk, but breast-feeding will offer him extra health benefits

HOWEVER YOU END UP feeding your baby, it's well worth starting off with breast-feeding. For a few days after the birth, your breasts produce colostrum, a substance rich in antibodies, so, by breast-feeding even for a few days, you can pass on protection against diseases to your baby.

Breast-feeding

Breast-feeding offers you and your baby tremendous health benefits. Antibodies in breast milk help protect your baby against illness in the early months, and breast-feeding also reduces the risk of your baby developing allergies. If there are allergies in your family, experts advise breast-feeding exclusively for at least four months, preferably six. The composition of breast milk alters week by week so it's always perfectly suited to your baby's changing nutritional needs. For mums, breast-feeding helps reduce the risk of breast cancer. It encourages your womb to contract and helps burn up fat laid down during pregnancy.

In terms of convenience, breast-feeding is hard to beat. Milk is always available at the right temperature, there's no equipment to

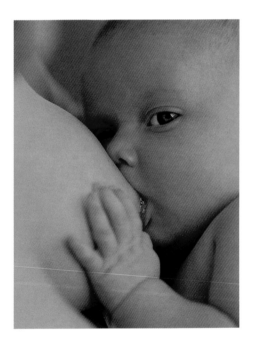

sterilise and no feeds to prepare ahead. It's also free. For many mums, breast-feeding is a rewarding and intimate experience.

Almost all healthy women are able to breast-feed, but it can take several weeks of perseverance to really get the hang of it. It can be exhausting, too. Some babies feed every two hours, and until you are able to express milk, only you can feed your baby.

Bottle-feeding

The advantages of bottle-feeding tend to be the opposite of the disadvantages of breast-feeding. For example, feeding can be shared with your partner and family right from the start. Bottle-fed babies tend to feed less frequently, so there are fewer interruptions to everyone's sleep. It's easy to feed your baby in public if necessary (it's possible with breast-feeding, too, but it takes a little more confidence). You can also see exactly how much milk your baby has had.

Although there are practical advantages, there are disadvantages, too. The most significant is that bottle-feeding provides none of the health benefits associated with breast-feeding. Also, when he's very young,

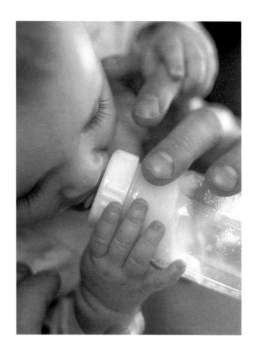

Feeding should be a relaxed and loving time when you and your baby get to know each other better

your baby may need seven or eight bottles a day. That means a lot of equipment to be sterilised, and advance planning to ensure there's always a bottle ready. Plus, buying formula and equipment makes bottle-feeding a more expensive option.

Which is right for you?

It's very important to give breast-feeding a try, because breast milk really does give your baby the very best start in life. If you start out breast-feeding and find it doesn't suit you, it's simple to then switch to the bottle. However, if you start off with bottle-feeding, it may not be possible to switch to breast-feeding later on.

If you find breast-feeding isn't working for you, for whatever reason, be reassured that your baby will thrive on formula, too. The most important thing is that you feel happy and confident about the way you're feeding. Whether you opt for breast or bottle, feeding should be a relaxed and loving time when you and your baby get to know each other better. If you have any problems, talk to your midwife or health visitor.

Breast-feeding

Good technique is the key to successful breast-feeding and, as with most things, practice makes perfect. Don't be surprised if it takes a while for you and your baby to perfect your skills

B REAST-FEEDING DOESN'T COME as second nature to everyone. You might take to it straight away or it may take you three or four weeks to really get the hang of it.

Your midwife will show you how to breast-feed. But, if you feel you need more support, contact your health visitor or a breast-feeding counsellor from La Leche League or the National Childbirth Trust (see pages 168-169) who can provide advice.

Your partner can make all the difference, too. Breast-feeding may look easy, but it takes up a lot of time and energy, and in the early weeks your baby may feed up to 12 times a day. Practical help that allows you to rest as much as possible will greatly improve your chances of success.

Getting started

It's important to get comfortable – at first your baby may want to feed for up to 20 minutes or more at a time. If you are sitting down, support your back with a cushion. Cradle your baby in your arm, with his body facing towards you, and use a pillow on your lap to take his weight and to bring him up level with your breasts. If you are

lying down, lie on your side and use pillows to get yourself comfortable. Lay your baby next to you, with his tummy against your ribs and his head in front of your breasts.

When you're ready, draw your baby towards you (rather than leaning towards him), so that his nose is in line with your nipple. Stroke his cheek with your nipple or with your finger and he should open his mouth wide and turn towards the nipple. This is called the rooting reflex. When his mouth is wide open, move him onto your breast so that your nipple and most of the areola (the coloured area around the nipple) are covered by his mouth.

One of the great things about breast-feeding is that you don't need any equipment – all it takes is you and your baby. However, you will need two or three maternity bras – get yourself measured for these about three weeks before you expect your baby. Breast pads, which you wear inside your bra, are good for absorbing leaks and keeping your nipples dry. Once feeding is established, you may want to buy a breast pump, steriliser and bottles so that you can express milk (see page 108).

What you need

Getting plenty of your breast into your baby's mouth is the key to allowing him to feed efficiently. If he has a good mouthful of breast, your baby actually pumps your milk out rather than sucks (it's sucking that will make your nipple sore). If it hurts once he starts feeding, your baby probably isn't 'latched on' correctly. Release the suction by inserting your little finger gently between his jaws (better than pulling your nipple out of his mouth, which is another cause of soreness), then try again.

As your baby begins to feed, you may experience a tingling sensation in your breasts as your milk flows to your nipples. This is referred to as 'let-down' and it is perfectly normal, although it is equally normal not to experience it.

How long for? How long you need to let your baby feed for depends very much on him. Some babies are guzzlers who empty the breast in five minutes, then let go of the nipple and fall asleep, content. Others take a swig, have a snooze, play with the nipple, then start again. Alternatively, you might have a comfort sucker who enjoys sucking for as long as possible, even after he's actually finished feeding. In general, once your milk supply is well-established (this can take a couple of weeks), your baby should not need to feed for longer than 30 minutes at a time. If he does take longer, it may mean that he isn't latching on properly and is having difficulty feeding efficiently. If this happens, ask your midwife or health visitor for advice.

One breast or two? Experts say it is best to let your baby drain one breast completely and then, if he is still hungry, finish up with a second course from the other. This is because your breasts produce two kinds of milk – a thirst-quenching foremilk, which is available each time your baby starts to feed, and a richer hindmilk, which follows. Allowing your baby to drain one breast first ensures he receives both types each time he feeds. Each time you feed your baby, begin with the opposite breast to the one you started with the last time.

How often? You should feed your baby as often as he wants. In the early days, this may be as much as 12 times in 24 hours, although the interval between feeds will gradually lengthen as the weeks pass. Don't try to get your baby into a routine. Letting him feed whenever he is hungry lets your body know how much milk it needs to produce to keep your baby happy.

Expressing your milk

Being able to express means that someone else can give your milk to your baby, either with a bottle or a spoon. However, it is best to wait until feeding is well-established – say three or four weeks – before giving it a try. The easiest way is to use either a manual or battery-operated pump. You can store expressed breast milk in the fridge for up to 24 hours or put it into special breast milk bags and freeze it for up to a month.

Breast-feeding queries

Can anyone breast-feed? In general, yes. The size of your breasts makes no difference and you can breast-feed even if you have inverted nipples, although you may need more help to get the hang of it. The only women who shouldn't breast-feed are those who've been advised against it because of health problems, such as HIV.

What can I eat and drink? You can eat whatever you like (although if there's eczema and asthma in the family, avoid peanuts). You'll need more calcium than usual – dairy products and canned fish are good sources – and you may feel thirstier, so drink plenty of water. You can drink alcohol but should drink less than two units a day and have at least one day off a week. Talk to your doctor or pharmacist before taking medication. Foods like onions, citrus fruits, coffee and chocolate may cause a reaction in a very few babies. If you think your baby may be affected, consult your GP.

When should I stop? You can continue to breast-feed for as long as you want – breast-feeding for at least four months helps ensure your baby receives the special health benefits of breast milk. When you do stop, give your milk production system a chance to wind down gradually. Replace one feed with a bottle or cup, then wait for three or four days before replacing another.

What about mixed feeding? Mixing breast and bottle isn't recommended for the first few weeks when you need to feed frequently to stimulate milk production. After this, many women give their baby an occasional bottle of formula. However, if you give regular bottles, your milk supply will be affected. As a result, if you want to return to full-time breast-feeding, you will need to breast-feed more frequently and for longer to increase your milk supply.

need to rest the sorest of the two for a couple of days to give it a chance to heal. Sometimes an infection can get into cracked nipples, which leads to mastitis.

Mastitis The first symptoms of mastitis may be a fever and feeling weak as if you have 'flu. A hard, red lump may appear on the breast. If you think you have mastitis, see your doctor immediately. The infection can be treated with antibiotics which are safe for your baby. It is normally best to continue feeding from the affected breast.

Common problems

It is not uncommon to experience a few problems when you start breast-feeding. Try not to be disheartened – you'll find that there's a lot of advice and support available to help you overcome them.

Sore nipples This is the most common problem for breast-feeding mums – especially at the beginning. Check with your midwife, health visitor or breast-feeding counsellor that your baby is correctly positioned on the breast – poor positioning is the main cause of sore nipples. Help prevent sore nipples by letting them dry in the air after each feed and changing breast pads frequently. If your nipples are sore, try wearing a loose, cotton t-shirt and going without a bra for short periods. If you are very sore, try a nipple shield. If your nipples become cracked and bleed, you may

Insufficient milk Provided you are healthy and you feed your baby whenever he lets you know he is hungry, you should be able to produce enough milk to meet his needs. However, if you are finding feeding difficult and your baby is not gaining weight, talk to your midwife. If feeding has been going well and your baby suddenly wants to feed more often, it could be that he is experiencing a growth spurt (common at ten days, a month and two months). Let him feed as often as he wants and the interval between feeds should settle down again.

Thrush If you have pink, shiny nipples and constant pain, you may have thrush, in which case there's a chance your baby may have it too – ask your doctor to check both of you. An antifungal cream may be prescribed for your nipples and your baby may need antifungal drops.

Bottle-feeding

Preparing your baby's bottles will quickly become part of your daily routine – but giving him his bottle can be a very special time when you both have a chance to cuddle up together

BOTTLE-FEEDING MEANS you'll need to decide which type of formula milk you want to use and buy equipment (see below) well before your baby arrives.

Formula milk is modified cows' milk with added vitamins and minerals. All brands have to comply with UK legislation on the amount of vitamins and minerals they contain, but the composition varies slightly. Once you've chosen one, stick with it – if you want to change, discuss it with your health visitor. Soya formula is available for babies allergic to cows' milk but don't use it unless advised by your GP or health visitor. Your baby needs about 150ml of milk per kilogram of body weight (2½fl oz per 1lb) every 24 hours. He won't drink the same amount at each feed, but gradually increase the amount in each bottle as he grows.

Making up a feed

● Wash hands, boil fresh water. Pour the required amount of water into a sterilised bottle. Add the appropriate scoops of milk, according to manufacturer's instructions.
● Level each scoop off with the back of a knife – never pack the powder down, heap the scoop high or add extra scoops. This will make the formula too concentrated which could be dangerous for your baby.

● **Bottles** Buy at least six standard or wide-neck bottles with caps, discs and lids. With wide necks, you can make the feed up in the bottle more easily, but you can fit more standard bottles into a steam steriliser.
● **Teats** You'll need at least eight teats. Anti-colic teats are designed to reduce the amount of air swallowed, teats with a cross-cut allow your baby to regulate the flow of milk himself, and natural teats help your baby imitate the sucking action at the breast.
● **Steriliser** Until your baby is at least six months old, his feeding equipment should be sterilised daily. Buy a steam or microwave steriliser, or sterilise by using sterilising tablets or by boiling. Bottle and teat brushes will help keep equipment really clean.
● **Insulated bottle carrier** This keeps bottles cool when you're out, but they should still be used within an hour. Ready-made formula in cartons needn't be kept cool if unopened, but once opened, use within an hour.

Bottles and **bits**

- Seal each bottle with a disc and a ring, and shake well so the powder dissolves.
- Remove the disks and rings, lying them on clean kitchen paper. Put a teat upside down in the neck of each bottle, making sure it doesn't touch the milk.
- Replace the discs and rings, put caps on and store in the fridge for up to 24 hours.

Giving a feed

- Wash your hands. Turn the teat in the bottle the right way round, then stand the bottle in a jug of hot water to heat the milk.
- Tip a little milk onto your wrist – it should be tepid and flow in a thin spray. If it fails to come out or flows very fast, replace the teat with another sterile one.
- Get comfortable and cuddle your baby close in a semi-upright position. Offer him the bottle and let him pull as much of the teat as he wants into his mouth.
- Make sure the teat is filled with milk so he's not swallowing air. Try loosening the ring around the neck of the bottle slightly to let air in and prevent the teat collapsing. Let your baby feed for as long as he wants.

Good hygiene

Cleaning and sterilising is vital to protect your baby from a severe tummy upset. Milk is easily contaminated by bacteria. **Before you sterilise** your bottles and teats, wash them thoroughly with warm water and washing-up liquid, using a bottle brush and teat brush. Rinse with clean water and dry with kitchen paper. **Once you've warmed** a bottle of milk up, use it within an hour. Any leftover milk must then be thrown away.

Moving on from milk

Once your baby reaches six months, milk will no longer meet all his nutritional requirements. Gradually you'll need to teach him how to eat real food and to show him what fun eating can be

MOST BABIES ARE READY for their first taste of real food between four and six months. If your baby is over four months, he may show you that he is ready to try his first 'solids' by watching intently as you eat and even making a grab for your food. Or he may seem hungry all the time and start waking again in the night for a feed when previously he had been sleeping through.

It isn't essential for your baby to start having solid foods until he is six months old. On the other hand, it is very important not to give your baby solids before the age of four months. His digestive system won't be ready and starting too early can lead to health problems later on, including a much higher risk of allergies.

If your baby is only three months old and seems to be hungry all the time, try feeding him more often if you are breast-feeding. If you're bottle-feeding, give your baby more milk or switch to a milk formulated for hungrier babies. Never make the formula more concentrated.

Equipment for weaning

For first tastes
- Weaning spoons or teaspoons
- Small weaning bowl
- Small bibs
- Food processor, hand-blender, liquidiser or mincer for puréeing food

From six months
- Highchair with harness
- Larger baby bowl
- Baby beaker
- Larger bibs

It is not necessary to sterilise your baby's eating utensils in the same way as you sterilise his bottles, but do make sure that they're kept very clean.

From four months

Baby rice is an ideal first food. You can also try steamed or boiled apple or carrot, puréed very finely with a liquidiser, hand-blender or mincer, and mixed with a little breast or formula milk or cooled, boiled water. You can also buy jars of puréed fruit and vegetables for babies which are suitable for first tastes. These first foods should have a runny consistency so that they are easy to swallow. When you're ready:

- Choose one of your baby's usual feed times to give him his first taste of solids. Some mothers opt for the evening when

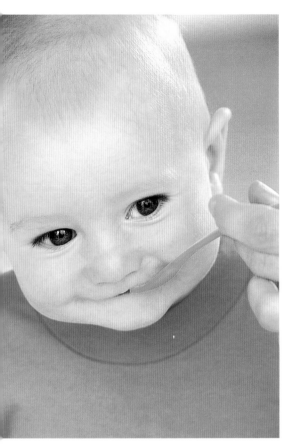

Introducing new tastes Once your baby is enjoying trying solid food, you can start to expand his menu, giving one food for a couple of days, then trying another for the next few. Until he's six months old, stick mainly to baby rice and puréed fruit and vegetables, prepared without salt or sugar. Your baby might enjoy apples, bananas, mangos, melons, peaches, pears, plums, avocados, broccoli, butternut squash, carrots, cauliflower, potatoes, pumpkin, swede and sweet potatoes. You can gradually introduce well-cooked, puréed meat too.

Don't worry if your baby refuses certain foods – try them again later on – it may take a while for his tastes to develop. Remember that, at this point, he is still getting all his nutrition from milk. You're simply encouraging him to enjoy the experience of eating. How he eats now isn't an indication of what kind of eater he'll be later on.

their breast milk supply is at its lowest, while others choose the morning when their baby is at his hungriest.

- Wash your hands. Give your baby half his normal feed to take the edge off his hunger. That way he'll be calmer when you offer him his first taste of solid food.
- Put your baby in a baby chair or prop him up in your arms and offer a tiny amount of food on the edge of a weaning spoon. These flat spoons are designed to make it easier for your baby to take the food. If he's unwilling to eat, don't force him. Try again a few days later. If he is eager, offer him a bit more. One teaspoon a day will be enough for the first few days. Finish off by giving him the rest of his usual milk.

Foods to avoid

Avoid giving the following foods to your baby until he's at least six months old. Some, like nuts, shouldn't be given until much later (see page 115):
- All dairy products
- All products containing gluten such as rye, barley and oats
- Wheat products, including bread, adult breakfast cereals, pasta
- Citrus fruits
- Sugar, salt and spices
- Eggs
- Honey
- Shellfish
- Nuts and seeds

Introducing more meals For the first couple of weeks of weaning, give your baby just one teaspoonful of solid food before one of his usual feeds, gradually building up to two or three teaspoons per feed. Then introduce solids before another feed, and then another, so that by the time he is six months old, your baby is having three 'meals' consisting of a few teaspoonsful of solid food a day before his milk. If you have a hungry baby, you may find that he'll eat a baby bowlful at one sitting.

By the time he is six months old, your baby's daily feeding routine might involve:
● A breast or bottle feed upon waking, followed by a breakfast of puréed baby rice or baby cereal made to packet instructions
● A milk feed as a mid-morning snack
● Lunch of a puréed vegetable, followed by dessert of a puréed fruit, and a milk feed
● A mid-afternoon drink of cool, boiled water from a training cup
● A milk feed at teatime plus a baby dish of well-cooked lean meat that's been finely-minced
● A milk feed before bedtime.

If you want to prepare fresh food for your baby, the easiest and most efficient way is to make up a batch of puréed vegetable or fruit, cool it, then freeze it in ice-cube trays. Put the frozen cubes in labelled bags with the date clearly marked (you can freeze fruit and vegetable purées for up to six months).

To serve, thaw however many ice-cubes you need, then heat the defrosted purée until piping hot to kill any harmful bacteria. Cool until tepid. Don't refreeze thawed meals or save uneaten food. Thawed food that hasn't been touched can be kept for up to 24 hours in the fridge.

For sheer convenience, commercially prepared baby foods are hard to beat, but they may work out to be more expensive than home-made food. They can provide a suitable diet for your baby, but it's good to give him fresh food too so that he can explore a wide range of tastes and textures.

When you choose a commercially prepared baby food, check that what you buy is suitable for your baby's age and read the ingredients carefully. Ingredients are listed in order of quantity, so a jar that has water at the top of the list, followed by carrots, contains more water than it does carrots.

Watch out for ingredients such as fructose, sucrose, glucose, maltose – they are all forms of sugar. And be aware that maltodextrin and emulsifiers are bulking agents which have little nutritional value.

If you are worried about the presence of genetically modified (GM) ingredients in shop-bought baby food, read the label, because some supermarkets have asked manufacturers to clearly label products that contain GM ingredients. If you want to be sure your baby's food is free from pesticides and additives, you could choose one of the several organic brands now on the market.

Home-cooked or ready-made?

From six months

After the age of six months, your baby can start to enjoy a much wider range of food. Although you still need to mash food, you no longer need to make it quite so fine. You can also now introduce:

● Dairy foods, such as yogurt and cheese. However, you should not switch to ordinary cows' milk as the main drink – stick with breast or formula milk. This is because cows' milk does not contain as much iron as breast or formula, and iron is a very important part of your baby's diet.

● Wheat-based foods, such as bread, pasta and unsweetened, fortified breakfast cereals.

● Eggs – but only well-cooked omelettes and hard-boiled eggs. You should avoid soft-boiled or undercooked eggs.

● Fish – take good care to remove all the bones and mash well.

● Soft fruits, such as cherries and apricots (stones removed), and citrus fruits.

You should still steer clear of nuts and seeds, salt and hot spices, honey, low-fat dairy products, soft, ripened cheeses such as Brie and Camembert, and foods which are either very fatty or very sugary.

From bottle to cup

When your baby is about six months old, the Health Education Authority recommends starting to wean him from his bottle to a cup, aiming to complete the process by the time he is a year old. **Teaching your baby** to drink from a cup, rather than suck a bottle, will help protect his new teeth (sucking from a bottle allows sugars to collect behind the teeth and rot them). If you are breast-feeding, it's fine to continue for as long as you want to, but if you wean your baby from the breast any time after six months, move him straight on to a trainer cup rather than a bottle.

As soon as your baby is comfortable eating in a highchair, introduce a trainer cup. Let him play with it and try to hold it, although he may need some help at first to drink from it. Praise him when he drinks well and don't moan about spills.

At six months, your baby will enjoy water (no need to boil) or fruit juice (diluted one part juice to ten parts water) as well as breast or formula milk – all from his cup.

When you introduce a new food, be aware of the risk of allergy. This is small, but symptoms could include vomiting, a rash, diarrhoea, eczema or swelling of the face. See your GP if you suspect a problem.

What your baby needs After the age of six months, solid food starts to rival breast or formula milk as the most important part of your baby's diet, although most babies will still need around 600ml (1 pint) of breast or formula milk a day until they are a year old. As solids gradually become an increasingly significant part of your baby's diet, you should aim to offer him as wide a variety of foods as possible to ensure that his nutritional requirements are being met.

Vegetarian babies

It is possible for babies to thrive on a vegetarian diet but, as protein and calcium are vital for healthy development, it's important that vegetarian babies receive a wide variety of cereals, beans and dairy produce every day.

From six months, mashed lentils, tofu, dairy foods and hard-boiled eggs can be introduced alongside cereals such as baby rice, corn meal, sago and millet.

Babies are born with their own store of iron. This is depleted by the time they are six months old. Babies raised on a vegetarian diet need plenty of iron-rich foods such as lentils, dried apricots, figs, egg yolks (well-cooked) and fortified cereals to make up for it. You should also give your baby plenty of vitamin C-rich foods, such as melon, kiwi, oranges and cauliflower, as these fruit and vegetables help with the absorption of iron.

If you are vegan and would like to raise your baby as one, it's best to consult your doctor or a dietician about your baby's dietary needs before you start weaning.

A balanced diet To help your baby to develop a healthy, balanced diet, offer him food from each of the following food groups every day:
● Milk and dairy foods, such as full-fat cheese, yogurt and fromage frais
● Meat, fish and protein alternatives, such as eggs, lentils, beans (including baked beans and chickpeas) and tofu
● Bread, potatoes, rice, pasta, maize and fortified, unsweetened breakfast cereal
● Fruit and vegetables, including dried fruits such as raisins and dried apricots.

Special requirements Babies need more fats and carbohydrates than adults, but it is better if they get these from full-fat dairy products and complex carbohydrates such as cereals and potatoes, rather than from sugary foods, such as biscuits and cakes, or fried food. Don't give your baby low-fat dairy products such as skimmed milk, diet fromage frais and reduced-fat spreads – he needs the vitamins and fat found in full-fat dairy products.

Babies do not need the same amount of high-fibre foods as adults do. Wholemeal bread, brown rice and very high-fibre cereals are very bulky and can prevent important minerals, such as calcium and iron, from being fully absorbed, so introduce them only gradually. If you are still breast-feeding after six months, your baby may need vitamin drops. Ask your health visitor for advice.

Learning to feed himself Between the ages of six and eight months, babies start to enjoy finger foods, such as slices of carrot or peeled cucumber, toast cut into fingers and bread sticks. These give your baby his first experience of independent eating, although it's important to keep an eye on him to make sure he doesn't choke. You can also start to let him experiment with a spoon, even if this means that most of his food ends up on his bib and face.

By the time he's nine months old, your baby will be able to eat a mashed-up version of many of your meals, provided they don't contain too much salt or sugar. This is a good time to let him join you at meal times so he learns that eating is a social occasion.

Happy eating Feeding can cause parents a lot of worry – especially when they start comparing their baby with someone else's. Never forget that – just like every adult – every child is different. Your job is to offer your baby a healthy variety of food and let him decide how much he wants and of what. Never try to force him to eat something he doesn't want – if he refuses a certain food, leave it and try to introduce it again at a later date. In the end, your baby is programmed for survival – left to his own devices he will choose food that meets his nutritional requirements. Don't worry if his appetite fluctuates. Some days he'll eat everything you put in front of him, other days, he'll hardly touch a thing.

Your baby's development

**Watching your baby grow is
one of the most rewarding
aspects of being a parent.
This chapter explains what
your baby will achieve in
the first year and shows
how you can help her along**

From newborn to toddler

During her first year, your baby will grow more quickly and learn more new skills than at any other time in her life. Your love and attention will play an important role in helping her to develop

DURING THE FIRST YEAR, your baby's brain triples in size, growing faster than any other part of her body. By her first birthday, her brain is already three quarters of its adult size – this gives you some idea of the huge developments in growth, mobility, understanding and speech that are in store.

Your newborn baby

A newborn baby seems helpless. She cannot even lift her own head, let alone walk and talk. Many of the connections between her brain cells, which will allow her to control her body and communicate in words, have yet to be made. Yet your new baby already understands the world in several ways. Within a few days of being born she can tell, by smell, your milk from other mothers' milk. She can focus up to 25cm (10in) away – which means she can see your face properly while she's feeding. And her hearing is well developed, too. She prefers rhythmic sounds (the sound of the washing machine, for instance) that remind her of the womb.

Your new baby also has several important reflexes – instinctive reactions designed to help her survive outside the womb. If you place your finger in her palm, she will grip it tightly. And if she is startled, she will throw out her arms and then draw them in to her body. Most importantly, her rooting reflex urges her to search out your nipple.

Within a few days, you can even see your baby beginning to learn by imitating you. If you poke your tongue out at her, you might find that she pokes her tongue out back.

Your baby at one

By the time your baby is a year old, she will be able to get about under her own steam. Some babies are walking by this stage, others are 'cruising' (walking sideways and holding onto furniture for balance), crawling or bottom shuffling. She'll also be able to express herself by pointing, making noises at a toy, smiling when she's pleased and crying when she's not. As well as giggling, shouting and squealing, she may even be saying 'mamma' or 'dadda'. She's starting to think about what she wants and how she can get it. She's aware of who the significant people are in her life and she loves to be with them. By now, she already has her own, very special, personality.

How your baby develops

As they move through their first year, all babies arrive at key developmental stages in the same order. Every baby, for example, learns to sit before she walks. However, each baby develops at her own pace. Often parents feel under pressure for their baby to reach a certain stage early or feel worried if she doesn't reach it right on cue. But these developmental stages are merely a rough guide. If your child says 'mamma' at ten months, it doesn't mean she'll be the next Einstein; similarly, if your baby isn't walking by the time she's one, it doesn't rule out a future career as an athlete.

If your child is happy and similar to other babies of the same age in most ways, and your GP and health visitor are satisfied with her development, don't worry too much. However, if you have a gut feeling that something is wrong, if your child has problems in her developmental tests (normally held at six to eight weeks, six to nine months and 18 months), talk to your GP or health visitor and ask to be referred to a specialist if necessary (see page 127).

Helping your baby learn Babies are born to play and be played with. For them, there is no distinction between playing and learning. At this stage of your baby's life, her most important toy and playmate is you, your partner or other family members and friends. Listening to you talking, watching you working and simply being with people are her favourite activities. She will enjoy playing with carefully chosen toys, too. But don't worry if you can't afford the latest, hi-tech activity set. They're good fun, but many generations of babies have grown up perfectly well without them.

Muscle power

Your baby is born with a walking reflex – hold her upright with her head supported and legs in contact with a surface and she'll make walking movements. However, over the first two months of life, this reflex fades. Her muscles are not yet developed enough to support her and

---

Your baby will progress at her own pace, but at these ages she may be able to:

At one month
- Lift her head when she's on her tummy

At four months
- Support her own head
- Raise her chest, using her arms, when she's on her tummy

At six to seven months
- Sit without support
- Take some of her weight on her legs when you hold her up

At eight to nine months
- Wriggle, crawl or bottom shuffle to get to an object that's out of reach

At one year
- Stand, using a prop, or 'cruise', using supports. A few babies can even walk.

First year milestones

allow her to walk properly. This is because they account for only a quarter of her weight whereas adults' muscles account for nearly half of their total body weight.

During the first weeks, your baby moves her arms and legs in what appears to be a series of random movements. In fact, she is doing a sort of 'work-out' that will eventually strengthen the muscles enough to allow her to move her body as she wants. She'll gradually gain control of her muscles, starting with those that support her head and progressing down her back to her legs.

Gaining head control It's not surprising that your baby can't support her head when she's born. It's enormously heavy compared with the rest of her, taking up a quarter of the length of her whole body. However, over the first couple of months, her neck muscles become strong enough to support her head, which allows her to really start looking around at the world.

Rolling The next big step for your baby is learning to roll over, which she may manage at around four months. Her first roll will probably be from her side onto her back. Some babies love rolling and will roll backwards and forwards almost non-stop. Others try the occasional roll, but don't ever turn over completely.

Sitting up Next on the agenda is sitting up, and it's harder than it looks. At first your baby may need to support herself with her arms. Make sure she's on a soft surface – surrounding her with cushions is a good tactic as there will be lots of toppling over. She'll slowly learn to sit up unsupported and will eventually be able to push herself up into a sitting position all on her own.

Crawling Many babies discover crawling some time between the age of six and ten months, as a result of falling over from sitting. They land on their hands and knees and discover that they can use this position to propel themselves along. Around one in five babies never crawls, either moving straight from sitting to walking, or preferring to shuffle along on her bottom.

Many crawlers go backwards before they go forwards. Some crawl at a sedate pace and others tear around the house. Some bumps are inevitable, but now that your baby is mobile, it is important to make sure that your home is a safe place for your baby to be (see box, right).

Walking Once your baby is crawling, it won't be long before she starts to pull herself up into a standing position. Once she's up, however, she may be unable to get down. It will take a while for her to work out that she needs to stick her bottom out and bend her knees for a soft landing.

The final stage before she starts to walk is 'cruising' – where she starts edging sideways, using the furniture and anything else that's handy as support. Cruising helps

your baby develop confidence to try her first steps and eventually to walk – perhaps as early as ten months or maybe later, a couple of months after her first birthday.

Try and let your baby develop at her own pace – walking requires lots of courage and co-ordination. Push-along trolleys can help, but don't rush her into a baby walker – they can be dangerous as they encourage speed and mobility that she is unable to control, and may slow down her developing sense of balance. Don't hurry her into shoes either. Let her practise walking barefoot at home before you add shoes to the equation.

Baby-proofing your home

It's vital to make your home safe as soon as your baby becomes mobile, as it's natural for babies to want to explore by crawling, touching and putting things in their mouths. Babies don't understand danger, so once your baby is on the move, the risk of accidents increases dramatically. Every year, half a million under-fives end up in hospital as a result of an accident in the home, so keep a close eye on your baby. Never leave her alone with an older child or pet and if you do leave her for a few moments, put her in a play-pen or cot. If your baby stays with relatives, make sure their home is safe, too.

Around the house
• Medicines (including vitamins and iron supplements), alcohol, cleaning fluids – lock them away in a high cupboard with a child-proof lock. Never decant chemicals into food containers (for example, white spirit in lemonade bottles).
• Cigarettes, matches and ashtrays – banish them from your home.
• Electrical appliances – they can be thrown into water or switched on. Don't leave them lying around.

• Knives, scissors, razors, pens, pencils, sewing and knitting tools, and plastic bags – can all be dangerous, so keep them locked away.
• Windows – fit window catches and keep chairs or tables away from windows to prevent your baby from climbing out. Tie back blind or curtain cords.
• Floors – polished ones can be slippery and dangerous.
• Buttons, beads, hard sweets, peanuts, coins and small parts on toys are all easily swallowed – keep them away from your baby.
• Fires – should always be covered with a fireguard.
• Electrical sockets – make them safe with safety covers.
• Stairs – fit stair gates at both the top and bottom.
• Trailing flexes on lamps – these make it easy for your baby to pull a lamp onto her head – get rid of them.
• Tables – fit safety pads over sharp corners.
• Changing mat – babies may push themselves off. Never leave your baby unattended on one.
• Hot drinks – don't try to drink them while you are holding your baby. Place all cups and mugs out of reach.
• Smoke alarm – fit at least one in your home and test it regularly.

In the kitchen
• Saucepans – put them on the back burner/ring and turn the handles away from the edge of the stove. Fit a stove guard if possible.
• Washing machine and tumble dryer – make sure your baby can't climb in.
• Kettle – models with a coiled flex which can't hang over the counter and be grabbed are safest.
• Tablecloths – these make it easy for your baby to pull the table contents on top of herself. Don't use them while she's around.
• Iron and ironing board – keep these well away from your baby.

In the bathroom
• Bath – put cold water in before hot to avoid scalding. Never leave your baby alone in the bath and empty it as soon as bathtime is over.
• Cosmetics (nail varnish remover, perfume) can be poisonous – lock them up.

In the garden
• Pools, ponds, buckets, paddling pools – empty them or cover them up.
• Garden chemicals and tools – keep them in a locked shed or garage.
• Plants – some are poisonous. If you've got any suspect species in your garden, pull them up.

Busy fingers

As humans, we are unique in the way we use tools in almost every aspect of our lives. For your baby, acquiring the skills she needs to use something as simple as a fork or pen is a tricky business. To reach for and grab an object, she'll need well-developed hand-eye co-ordination and to be able to estimate the size, weight and texture of the object so that she can adapt her grasp accordingly. Toys can play an important role in helping your baby to develop these skills (see below).

Reaching At first your baby's hand movements will be very uncontrolled – the only thing she seems capable of doing is putting her fists into her mouth, and even that seems to happen by accident. By around three months, however, your baby can actually reach for things that interest her. Lie her under a baby gym and you will see her gaze intently at the dangling objects and then swipe out in an effort to reach one. A rattle or a mobile just out of reach will provoke the same reaction – even your nose or a necklace will become fair game.

Grasping It is only a short step from reaching to grasping. This happens at about four months when your baby finally manages to grab and shake her rattle. After a few shakes, she'll probably put it in her mouth. This doesn't mean she wants to eat it – it's just that her mouth is very useful for exploring. By about six months, she may be able to hold a spoon well enough to start trying to feed herself, although an imperfect aim means that most of her food is likely to end up in her hair or all over the carpet.

Toys play an important role in helping your baby develop manual dexterity and hand-eye co-ordination. Always give her toys appropriate for her age and check that they carry the CE mark.
From 0 to 6 months
• Show her picture books with simple images in strong, contrasting colours.
• Hang an interesting object just beyond your baby's grasp to encourage her to reach for it. Baby gyms are perfect for this.

• Shake a rattle or other musical toy in front of her and encourage her to make a grab for it.
• Give her toys of different sizes, shapes, colours and textures. Don't overwhelm her with a pile of toys – give her a few at a time. Playmats also provide colours and textures to explore.
From 6 to 12 months
• Show her how stacking beakers fit inside each other and build towers for her to knock down.

• Give her raisins or pieces of chopped-up apple to help her practise the pincer grip.
• Let her play with bits of pastry and water to explore different textures.
• Give her a ball or toy bean bag, then encourage her to pass it back to you.
• Introduce her to toys with buttons and knobs to grab, push and turn, especially ones where pushing a button makes something happen.
• Give her a drum to make noises – if you can stand it.

Learning through play

Babies with **special needs**

Every child develops at a different rate. However, a few babies have problems which mean that their development may be slow or restricted, and they may need special help to reach their full potential. Some conditions, such as a cleft palate, are apparent at birth (or even in the womb) and may be treatable. But others, such as spina bifida and Down's syndrome, are permanent. There are also conditions, such as hearing problems, which may not be picked up until your baby undergoes routine checks during her first year.

If your baby has been diagnosed as having special needs, you may react in a number of ways. You may feel shock, disbelief, fear, anger and helplessness – all normal reactions. Sometimes, when the doctor tells you for the first time that there's a problem, you may not be able to take it all in. If this is the case, don't be afraid to go back to the doctor. Take a notebook with you and ask any questions you have written down and make notes. If you find your specialist to be unhelpful, ask to see another.

One of the major problems for parents of children with special needs is isolation, but there are organisations that can help (some are listed on pages 168-169). Ask your doctor for details of support organisations who can put you in touch with other families in a similar situation. They can also provide practical help and advice on claiming extra benefits or helping you to find a qualified baby-sitter so you can enjoy a break. If your child's problem is not too serious, it may be relatively easy for you to adjust. However, if the condition is severe, it can be hard to come to terms with. Try to be reassured that, with time and help, most families do manage to adjust.

Once your baby has mastered grabbing and holding, she starts to refine these skills, experimenting with smaller objects and eventually learning to use her thumb and her first finger (known as the pincer grip) to pick up something as small as a raisin. This is the skill she'll need eventually to be able to do up her clothes or write with a pen.

Making things happen As your baby starts to gain control over her body, she will learn that she can use it to make things happen. She pushes a button on a toy, for example, and it makes a ringing sound, or she holds her beaker over the edge of her high chair, releases her grip and hears it go clattering to the floor.

Speech and sounds

Babies are sociable creatures. Experiments show that even nine days after birth they can distinguish their own language from a foreign one. However, actually learning to communicate through speech takes time.

Crying is the first way your baby learns to attract your attention and to show pain or discomfort. However, by six weeks, your baby will probably smile in response to your smile – some experts have even speculated that the smile appears when parents are at their most exhausted, in order to re-establish the love they feel for their baby.

By eight weeks, your baby will have other ways of communicating. Raise your eyebrows at her and she may raise hers back. She will also start to make cooing sounds and, by the end of four months, will be squealing and laughing. A few months later, she will begin to blow raspberries.

and understand the meaning of simple words such as 'bath' or 'shoe'. It's around this time that she'll say her first 'proper' words – which are most likely to be 'mamma' or 'dadda'. She may even try to fill the gap in a conversation by making sounds.

Helping your baby talk The best way to help your baby develop her language skills is to talk to her. Most of the time, just talking about what you're doing or where you're going is enough, but don't forget to turn the radio or television off as she will be able to concentrate better if there is no background noise.

Start with simple sentences with lots of repetition, such as: "Look at the cat. It's a lovely soft cat." If your baby starts to babble, copy it and add something else for her to copy as well – for instance, imitate a squeal and add: "lovely squeal". Try to

By the time your baby reaches her first birthday, she will recognise her name and understand simple words

Sounds like laughter are a complete form of expression in themselves, but other sounds your baby makes are practice for speaking. Studies show that, although babies begin to babble to their mothers at around six months, they also practise making sounds even when there's no-one to hear. By the time your baby reaches her first birthday, she will be able to recognise her own name

make a time every day to really concentrate on talking to her to encourage her language skills. Babies enjoy books from a very early age so look at books together and talk about the pictures. Sing nursery rhymes – she'll love the actions that go with them and will soon join in. If this happens, praise her. It's important to tell her how clever she is when she does something new.

Your new life

From the moment your
baby is born, life will
never be the same again.
This chapter explores the
challenges and changes
you'll face as a new mum

Taking care of yourself

Now that your baby is born, you're probably keen to get your body back into shape. But life with a new baby is hectic, so eat well, exercise gently and take things one step at a time

BEFORE YOU GAVE BIRTH, you might have imagined that you would regain your figure almost immediately. However, it can take up to a year for your body to get back to normal. For now, your breasts will be fuller and your tummy may sag. Any stretch marks or a caesarean scar will also take quite a while to fade. You may find that, when your weight finally settles, you're a few pounds heavier than you used to be. You can get back into shape, but it's best to take it gently at first.

Eat well

Dieting is not advised in the early months if you are breast-feeding. Even if you are not breast-feeding, life is tough enough for the first few months anyway, without the strain of dieting. However, you can, and should, eat as healthily as you can.

- Base meals on carbohydrates such as bread, potatoes, pasta and rice. These supply energy, which means you'll be less tempted to fill up on snacks.
- Have at least five helpings of fruit and vegetables a day. Don't eat too many sugary foods such as biscuits, sweets and cakes.
- You'll need some protein each day – that's meat, fish, eggs, dairy produce such as milk and cheese, and lentils and beans.
- Cut down on fats. Bake or grill food instead of frying, and choose lean cuts of meat. Opt for reduced-fat foods such as skimmed milk and half-fat cheese.

After **a difficult birth**

If you have gone through a really tough birth, perhaps with the full range of intervention and a medical emergency to top it all, you may well feel shocked and shaky. Getting information is important. You need to know what went wrong and why, and whether precautions can be taken to stop this happening again if you have another baby. Talk to the hospital, your GP and your midwife. Let your GP know if you are suffering panic attacks or depression, as these can be treated. Above all, be kind to yourself. Arrange as much help as you can. You will recover, but it will take longer than it would if you had had an easy birth, and you will need extra support and understanding from those closest to you.

Take gentle exercise

Exercise is a great way to relieve stress and shape up. The easiest exercise to fit in with a new baby is walking. Try and take regular, brisk walks with the pram, standing tall with your shoulders back, your bottom tucked under and your tummy pulled in. You should also do pelvic floor exercises every day. Remember, too, that your ligaments will still be soft for three to six months after you've given birth, so carry on taking care of your back (see pages 18-19).

If you decide to join in an exercise class, let the instructor know that you have just had a baby (especially if you have had a caesarean) as some exercises may be unsuitable.

Exercising at home In the early days, tone up at home with these floor exercises. Start off with three or four repetitions, gradually doing more as you feel stronger.

Pelvic tilt Lie on your back with your feet flat on the floor and knees bent. Pull in your stomach muscles and bottom, and press the small of your back firmly against the floor. Hold for a count of three. Relax.

Head lift Keep your knees bent and the small of your back pressed against the floor. Rest your hands beside you and breathe in. As you breathe out, gently lift your head and shoulders. Hold for a count of three, then lower your head and shoulders to the floor, breathing in as you relax.

Leg slide Still lying on the floor, stretch both legs out straight. Slide one foot up towards your bottom, keeping the other leg straight. Make sure the small of your back is pushed against the floor. Slide your foot down and repeat with the other leg.

Rest and relax

Finding time to rest and relax is just as important as exercising – and if, in the early weeks, you can't fit in both, resting should come top of your list. Put some other parts of your life on hold for a while and use the time to sleep, rest in front of the television, listen to music, go for a massage or to do whatever calms you best.

Your relationship

Your new baby will have a huge impact on your relationship with your partner. The early months can be tough, but they are also a time when you can show your love and support for each other

ONE THING IS CERTAIN when you have a baby. Whatever your relationship with your partner was like before, it will be different after. The two of you are now more than just partners. You're parents, too – and a third person has joined your relationship. While it's widely believed that having a baby can bring a couple together, it's less recognised that a baby is just as likely to widen any existing rift or even to create one.

Adjusting to the changes

It might sound gloomy, but the fact is that if you find yourself snapping at your partner more than usual, feeling completely uninterested in sex and arguing more, this is perfectly normal. Sleepless nights, exhaustion, financial worries and not much time to yourselves don't make for either good temper or a brilliant sex life. It doesn't mean that your partnership will not come through. Most marriages and long-term partnerships do survive this period.

If you've always prided yourself on how evenly balanced your relationship is, it might take quite some readjustment if you find that, as a mum, you are taking on the lion's share of the baby care and domestic tasks while your partner concentrates on paid work. If you both go back to work full-time, you may find you're both so exhausted with working and looking after your baby that your relationship gets neglected. If you end up working full-time and still being responsible for the home, you're likely to feel resentful – and with reason.

Relationships that come through this challenging time strengthened, rather than fractured, are those where the woman feels that her partner supports her both emotionally and practically. Not surprisingly, those relationships where the man continues to live his life as if the baby had not been born, do not do so well.

Keep your relationship alive

Remember that the first year of a baby's life is a tough time for many parents. Things will get better if you can just hang in there.
● Make time for each other. A night out together each week is a marvellous tonic. (See box on baby-sitters on page 137.) It needn't be elaborate, but it should be a time when you can talk – and laugh – together.

• Keep talking. If you can explain your feelings to your partner, it will help him understand what you're going through and reduce the risk of misunderstanding. You cannot expect your partner to mind-read.

• Don't expect to be able to carry on just as you did before your baby was born. This may be a time when hobbies, friends and a social life need to take second place to your commitment to each other.

• Be sympathetic to each other's point of view. A man should understand that, for a woman, being a mother takes precedence over being a lover in the early days. A woman should understand that her partner needs to feel loved as well as the baby.

• In these early months, you should be as kind to yourself as possible. Be prepared to drop your standards on housework, cooking, entertaining – in short, don't try to be the all-round perfect wife-daughter-mother. Make sure that you have at least half an hour each day to yourself. You are more likely to be sympathetic to your partner and his needs if you feel that your own needs are being met.

• Be appreciative of your partner and express that appreciation.

• Families can be a source of great support, but they can also be a source of stress. If your family is helpful, relish that help. If they are actively hostile to your partner, critical of your child-rearing methods or very demanding, they may need to take a back seat for the next couple of months.

● Don't be afraid to ask for help if it isn't offered – friends and family are often only too glad to provide support.

● Try to involve your partner in baby care in a positive way. Don't criticise his efforts even if you can do something better and faster than he can.

● This is not the best time to plan other huge changes in your life such as moving house or taking on a challenging new job. Try to put a little time between the birth of your baby and other major upheavals.

● If you feel that your relationship is suffering and that you could benefit from some outside help, try contacting a counselling service such as Relate (see page 169).

Sex after the birth

You can start having sex again as soon as you feel like it after the birth, although some women prefer to wait until after their six-week check. However, even after six weeks, you may find that your sex drive is low. This is quite normal and some scientists have even speculated that it is nature's own contraceptive.

Stay physically affectionate towards one another with hugs, stroking, massage and kissing. You may need to be reassured that you are still attractive to your partner. Or you may feel your partner is finding it difficult to readjust to you as a mother as well as a lover. Talking things through will help.

If you feel like sex, but sex itself is painful or lacks sensation, talk to your GP about it. Sometimes breast-feeding can make the

---

Looking after a new baby is tough, but looking after a new baby on your own is tougher. As a lone parent, it's important that you look after yourself and your well-being. Your baby relies on you and a happy mother makes for a happy baby. If you split up with your partner during your pregnancy or after the birth, you may feel emotionally vulnerable and, in this case, getting support is even more important.

● **Don't be frightened** of asking for help – parents and friends can all be good sources of support. Try to arrange for someone to come round or take your baby out once a week so you can catch up on sleep.

● **Try to join** a mother-and-baby group, NCT group or a group for single parents,

such as Gingerbread (see page 168), which can all provide you with the opportunity to make friends with other parents.

● **Make sure** you're getting the benefits you are entitled to as a single parent. Your benefits office or Citizens Advice Bureau should be able to help. If you were working before the birth, you may well find that by going back you can ease both isolation and money worries, the two biggest problems for single parents. Make sure that your baby's father is paying his share – your Citizens Advice Bureau can provide further advice on this.

● **Look for** exercise and other classes that have crèche facilities. Your local library will probably have details.

If you're a single parent

Finding a **baby-sitter**

Choosing someone to look after a very small baby is a difficult task. A trusted relative or friend is clearly the best solution, but there are other options.

• **Some organisations** such as local NCT branches run baby-sitting circles where parents take it in turns to baby-sit for one another. This can be a good way of making friends and finding baby-sitters, but you need to be willing to take your turn at baby-sitting, too. Alternatively, other women in the group may be able to recommend someone.

• **Local nurseries** that care for babies may have qualified childcarers willing to undertake baby-sitting. Your health visitor may also know of someone.

• **However you find** a potential baby-sitter, always ask for two references that you can take up by phone. Ask if your baby-sitter has first-aid training. If not, buy a first-aid manual and leave it for her. Always give your baby-sitter a contact number where you can be reached, an emergency number and your doctor's number. It's best to agree fees in advance.

• **The first time** you use a baby-sitter, go out somewhere close by for just a couple of hours. Make sure the baby-sitter knows everything she needs to about your baby's routine, especially his bedtime routine, and your ideas on baby care.

vagina drier than normal and you may need extra lubrication, such as a water-based gel. Be aware, too, that it is possible to get pregnant as soon as you have unprotected sex after the birth, even before you have had your first period. If you do not want to become pregnant, you need to use contraception. If you want to take the pill and are breast-feeding, you will need to use the mini-pill, rather than the combined pill. If you are not breast-feeding, it's OK to use the combined pill. However, the pill may not be suitable if you are suffering from post-natal depression. Other reliable options include the condom (male or female), a diaphragm or an IUD, which will need to be fitted. Talk to your doctor or family planning clinic for more information.

Above all, remember that when it comes to sex, quality matters as much as quantity and that things generally do get better.

A new way of life

Having a baby means a whole new lifestyle, but it's not one that comes ready-made. Like all new mums, you'll need to work out for yourself a way of life that suits you, your partner and your baby

BECOMING A PARENT is a major life change and it's bound to inspire mixed feelings. The joy of cuddling your baby is hard to beat but that doesn't mean you won't yearn for your old life when you had more sleep, more time and more money.

Happy families?

Society likes to depict the ideal of the perfect family where everyone is smiling every minute of the day. This family doesn't exist. In fact, there is no such thing as the perfect parent either. Every parent has days when things go well and everyone has off days, too. And unlike work, where you have daily goals, parenting is a long-term project and changes happen only gradually.

There isn't only one right way to bring up a child and you'll learn through trial and error what suits your baby best. In the meantime, you need to work out a way of life that is satisfying (not perfect) for you and your family, and it may mean making adjustments such as taking on less at work.

Becoming a parent often strengthens existing family relationships. You may find, for example, that your mum or mother-in-law is a great source of support. On the other hand, you may want to see less of those people whose only contribution to your parenting effort is to criticise.

All change

Most people understand that becoming a mother is a huge change for a woman. But parenthood is a big change for a man, too. He suddenly becomes responsible for a new little person and may feel uncertain of his role, be weighed down by new financial pressures or mourn the fact that he no longer has his partner solely to himself. Understanding that you are both going through change – and trying to ride it together – can help. Although postnatal depression in women is widely recognised, there is now evidence to suggest that men can suffer from it, too.

If you have had twins or more, the adjustments you will have to make to your life will be even greater. For practical advice and support, it may help to contact a national organisation like TAMBA (see page 169) who have groups for parents of twins all around the country.

Meeting other parents

When you become a parent your priorities change. Your sore nipples may suddenly become a cause of greater concern than the 'who's going out with who' gossip or the in-depth 'what the boss said' discussions. If your social circle includes people who are also new parents, you may find them a great source of support. But, if your friends are footloose and fancy-free, they may not be interested in the fact that your baby slept through the night last night. And you may not care that they've been out clubbing until 3am. If your friends are interested in your new life and you in theirs, the friendship will survive. However, you may also find that you need some new friends.

Where to find them There are lots of ways to meet other new parents including mother-and-baby groups, one o'clock clubs, church groups and National Childbirth Trust postnatal groups. Many local authority fitness centres have classes with a crèche – indeed, any activity with a crèche is a good way to meet other parents. Your local library or health visitor should have a list of groups in your area. If you work, you may have less time, but if you want to talk to people who share your experience, try joining a group for working parents, such as those run by Parents At Work or the National Childbirth Trust (see page 169).

A holiday with your baby

If you can afford it, a holiday with your baby is a great way to relax. It doesn't need to be elaborate – in fact, it's best to stick to short journeys and flights. Consider the following points, too:

• If you choose to go self-catering, check that the premises are suitable for babies and take essential safety equipment with you, if necessary. Avoid anywhere with an unfenced pond or pool, an open fireplace, busy roads and lots of steep steps.

• Your baby must have his own passport, including a photo of him without you.

• Make sure you have holiday insurance that covers your baby as well as you and your partner. Read the small print.

• If travelling outside Europe and the US, check the vaccination requirements. Some vaccines are not suitable for babies.

• Pack a baby first aid kit, sun hat, insect repellent, water wings, lots of wipes and a few disposable bibs.

• Take your own car seat or hire one, but if you hire, make sure the seat meets safety standards and is fitted properly.

• If travelling to Europe or the US, you'll be able to buy jars of familiar baby food, but take your baby's favourites as back-ups.

• Pack feeding, expressing and sterilising equipment if necessary. If you pack a steriliser, check it can be adapted to work in the country you are visiting. Alternatively, for an easy-to-carry option, buy a travel kit containing sterilising tablets and strong plastic bags.

• In hot countries, good food hygiene is very important to prevent tummy upsets.

• Keep your baby covered (in a t-shirt and hat) and in the shade. Apply factor 20+ sun-screen regularly to any areas of the skin that are uncovered.

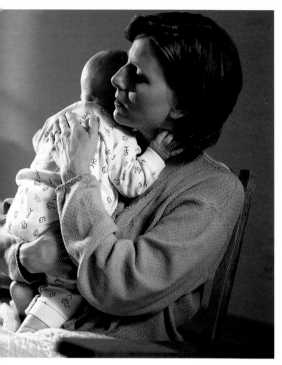

Postnatal depression

About one in ten new mothers experiences postnatal depression (or PND) to some degree. It affects women of all ages and backgrounds, and no-one is sure why. Some theories link it to hormonal imbalance and others suggest a psychological condition affecting, in particular, women who have relationship or financial worries and those with unresolved issues in their own lives.

Symptoms Caring for a baby is hard work. Like most mums, you'll probably feel exhausted and moody but there will be days when you enjoy your baby and feel on top of things. If there aren't and you are feeling down most of the time, you may be suffering from PND. The symptoms are:

● Feeling exhausted all the time. You may find it hard to settle to sleep, be unable to go back to sleep once woken, or wake early.

● Feeling weepy, sad or numb much of the time or having bouts of crying that you can't really explain.

● Frequent feelings of anger either with yourself, your baby, your partner or everyone. Being constantly irritable.

● Feeling unable to cope and thinking that you are the only one who isn't coping.

● Feeling guilty at what you perceive is your 'failure' to be the perfect mother.

● Showing a lack of interest in activities you would normally enjoy such as sex, food, shopping and socialising.

● Feeling constantly anxious about your baby or life in general, and feeling that your baby would be better off without you or wanting to harm your baby.

Seeking help If you are suffering from PND, it is not your fault. Like so many other illnesses, it is just something that happens and it's treatable. However, to get treatment you must first seek help. Most GPs will be sympathetic. Admitting that you are not feeling yourself does not mean that you will be judged and found wanting. Seeking help is in your baby's best interests as well as yours – a happy mother is better than a miserable one.

If your depression has been partially triggered by lack of support, it may be useful to contact Home-Start which offers support to mothers. You can also contact other PND sufferers via The Association for Postnatal Illness (see page 168).

Returning to work

The decision whether to return to work or not is a very personal one. If you do go back, being happy with the type of child care you choose will help you make the most of your working day

SOONER OR LATER, new mothers have to decide whether to return to work or not. This decision could come within three or six months of your baby arriving, depending on how long you've been employed. Whatever you decide, talk things through with your partner first.

Making the decision

There are several issues that will affect your decision whether to return to work or not. Key points to consider include:

Income Don't forget to take into account tax, child care and travel costs when you work out how much you'll be bringing home. If your family has a relatively low income, you may be able to get help with child care costs – ask at your local Citizens Advice Bureau or benefits office for details.

If you are the main wage earner (as one in five women now is) or a single parent, the decision to return to work may be cut and dried. But, if your partner is the major breadwinner and child care is likely to eat up your income, you may decide returning to work full-time is not worthwhile.

Job satisfaction Some women love being at home and are happy to take on the nurturing role. Others feel bored and need the camaraderie of the workplace and the feeling of daily achievement that work brings. If this sounds like you, there's no need to feel guilty, or let others make you feel guilty, about going back to work. If you are happy, the chances are that your happiness will spread to your child. It is better to be a contented working mother than a miserable stay-at-home one. If you plan to work, it's important to find good child care.

Flexible working options If you need an income but could manage on less money, or if you enjoy your job but want to spend more time with your baby, then part-time or flexible working, or job-sharing could be an option. It's worth approaching your employer to see if you can work something out that's beneficial to you both. In a few cases, refusing to allow a woman to change her hours may be against sex discrimination law. Contact the Maternity Alliance (see page 169) if you feel your employer is being unreasonable.

Your partner's opinion If you return to work, is your partner willing to share the domestic chores? If you stay at home, is he willing to take on the financial burden? The advice of friends and relations on this matter, unless practical (such as offering help with child care), should not influence your decision. This is a matter for you, your partner, your child and your employer.

Child care The quality and cost of child care available will have a big influence on your decision. If you can go to work safe in the knowledge that your baby is well cared for, you'll be able to keep your mind on the job. But if you are unhappy about the quality of care he's receiving, it is unlikely that you will be productive or happy at work.

Arranging child care

If you do decide to go back to work, finding suitable child care will be a priority. There are a wide range of options available.

Child minders This is the most popular form of paid child care. A child minder is often a parent herself and looks after her own and other children in her home. She has to be registered with her local authority which means that she's undergone basic police checks, her home has been checked for safety and she has insurance. Apart from care by a relative, a child minder is often the cheapest child care option.

The advantages of using a child minder include the fact that your baby has a home-from-home at the child minder's house where he'll get to mix with other children early on. If the arrangement is successful, your child minder may be willing to take your baby through to school age and beyond, giving your child a considerable degree of stability. Some child minders are happy working part-time or flexible hours.

But there are disadvantages. You will have to get your baby ready and to the child minder's house before you set off for work. The child minder may have her own routine and your baby will have to fit in with it. If your baby or child minder is sick, you will need to find alternative care but may still be expected to pay. You may also be expected to pay during your own or your child minder's holidays.

Choosing a child minder You can find out about registered child minders in your area through your local authority or via the National Childminding Association (see page 169). Interview any candidate in her own home and at length. Look around. Ask to meet her children and partner, if he's living at home. Has she looked after babies before. Can she supply references? Ask to see registration and insurance documents. What other children is she looking after? Does she hold a first aid certificate? What's her daily routine? Does she smoke? Discuss your ideas about bringing up children and arrange a trial day before making a final decision.

Relatives Partners are the most popular form of child care in Britain today, closely followed by grandparents. The biggest advantage of having a relative looking after your baby is that he will be cared for by someone you know and who has his best interests at heart. It's also cheap (or free) and usually flexible.

But it's not without its drawbacks. You will have a more emotional relationship with your baby's carer and may not agree completely about how he should be raised. If your hours increase or you're often late, a relative may feel resentful. If your partner becomes a full-time carer, he may feel isolated. Beware of a continual shift rota – one coming in from work as the other leaves – this places a strain on your relationship.

Making it work Set the ground rules before you finalise the arrangement. This may include agreeing what your baby is to eat and a daily routine, including nap times. If a relative is looking after your baby free of charge, find a way to thank her for her help, whether it's paying for a treat or a day out, or cooking a meal.

Nursery There are different types of nursery, including workplace, private and local authority. Private nurseries are generally more expensive than a child minder but cheaper than a nanny. Some local authority nurseries are free or subsidised.

The main benefit of a nursery is that your baby will be looked after by trained carers and, provided that staff turnover is low, he will enjoy continuity of care. He will be able to take part in a wide range of stimulating activities and mix with other children from an early age.

But, as with child minders, you will have to get your baby to the nursery before you set off for work and you won't be able to take him when he is sick. Opening hours are rigid. If the nursery closes at 6pm, you will need to be there at 6pm, no matter what, and there are often long waiting lists for very few nursery places.

for two years; others just have experience of looking after children. Nannies are the most expensive option, although live-in nannies generally cost less than live-out ones. A nanny-share, where your baby spends some days at your home and some at another family's, is a less expensive arrangement.

With a nanny, your baby has one-to-one care. Many nannies don't mind long hours, but the quality of care varies and some nannies like to change jobs frequently, so you're not guaranteed continuity of care.

The quality and cost of child care will have a big influence on whether you decide to work or not

Choosing a nursery Contact your local authority's children's unit for a list of nurseries in your area. Arrange a visit to find out about a typical day at the nursery. Check the qualifications of staff and the staff turnover. Does the nursery run a system where one staff member (known as a 'key worker') will be responsible for and have a special bond with your baby? Does it feel like a happy place? What activities will your baby be able to take part in as he grows? Visit a few times before choosing.

Nanny or nanny-share A nanny is a carer who looks after your children in your own home, and may or may not live with you. Some are qualified – an NNEB certificate means a nanny has studied child care

Choosing a nanny You can find nannies through agencies, word-of-mouth and publications such as 'Nursery World' or 'The Lady'. The National Childbirth Trust also keeps registers of nanny-shares.

Interviewing prospective nannies carefully is crucial – ask the same questions as you would of a child minder (see page 144). Don't rely on written references – call referees and get as much information as you can. Ask whether they'd employ the nanny again. Check out her qualifications and any gaps in employment history. If you like a nanny and she has good references, arrange for her to meet your baby to see how they interact before offering the job. If you employ someone, make an unscheduled visit home to check all's well.

Your baby's health

Taking care of your baby's
health is quite different to
taking care of your own.
This chapter provides basic
information on everything
from common colds to
rare accidents, to help you
see your baby safely
through her first year

When your baby is ill

For most babies, being ill will mean nothing worse than having a cold – and although even this can be worrying, your doctor should be able to provide reassurance as well as medical advice

BEING RESPONSIBLE for a tiny new baby and her health can be daunting, especially at first when you still have very little experience of what 'normal' is for her. However, your health visitor and your GP are there to share the responsibility – perhaps the most important part of your job is to know when to ask for their advice.

Is my baby ill?

Sometimes, when your baby is ill, she may have very obvious symptoms, such as a temperature or vomiting. At other times, there won't be any particular symptoms –

you may simply notice that she is not quite herself. Babies who are ill often become listless and lose interest in what's going on around them, while babies who are in pain may become sad and withdrawn.

If you think that your baby may be sick, trust your instincts and contact your GP. Many doctors will see a mother with a young baby at short notice and taking your baby to the surgery, rather than waiting for a home visit, will often be the quickest way to get medical advice. Outside surgery hours, all surgeries have arrangements for you to speak directly to a doctor by phone.

Meningitis is a relatively rare condition, but if your baby is affected, it's vital to recognise the symptoms as early as possible so you can seek immediate medical treatment. You should be aware that your baby may not show all of these symptoms at one time:
• Refusing her feeds or being sick
• High-pitched moaning cry or whimpering

• Being fretful and not wanting to be picked up
• A bulging fontanelle (the soft spot on the top of your baby's head)
• A tendency to arch her head and neck backwards
• Blank, staring expression
• Difficult to wake and has no energy
• Pale and blotchy skin
• A reddish/purple skin rash which doesn't become white when pressure is

applied (to test, see below). It can appear anywhere – even behind the ears or on the soles of the feet.
The tumbler test can be used to check whether a skin rash could be a sign of meningitis. Place the side of a glass tumbler against the skin over the rash and press gently – the rash should disappear. If it doesn't, you should seek urgent medical advice.

Symptoms of meningitis

Is it an emergency?

If your baby has any of the symptoms below, call your doctor or the emergency services immediately, or take your baby straight to the nearest GP's surgery or a hospital with an Accident and Emergency department. If necessary, give emergency first aid (see pages 152-157) before you leave.

● Your baby is unconscious, drowsy, difficult to rouse or floppy:

– as a result of dehydration following a bout of diarrhoea and/or vomiting,

– during a feverish illness,

– after a fit (unless she's had them before and you know what to do) or after a fall.

● Your baby has a breathing problem:

– her breathing is fast and shallow (and especially if she is limp or pale),

– breathing is clearly an effort for her,

– she has blueness around the lips.

● Following an accident or fall:

– if you suspect a head or limb injury,

– if your baby has anything other than the most minor cuts, burns or scalds.

● If you think she has swallowed something poisonous, such as:

– cleaning liquids, adult medicines or pills,

– harmful plants from the garden,

– a battery from a watch or hearing aid which may contain mercury.

Your baby's temperature

A raised temperature is often the first sign of illness in babies, although it's important to be aware that your baby can be ill even if her temperature is normal.

Taking a temperature The easiest way to test your baby's skin temperature is by placing your cheek or the back of your hand against her forehead. You will soon be able to recognise when her temperature is different from usual. However, a thermometer will allow you to take her temperature more accurately and also to track whether it is rising or falling. There are several types:

● Digital thermometer: this needs to be placed under your baby's arm for a minute or two to give a reading. Digital thermometers are not the cheapest option, but they are tough and reliable. Don't forget to keep a spare battery handy.

● Temperature indicator strip: this is a heat-sensitive plastic strip which you place against your baby's forehead – colours on the strip change to show her temperature. The strips are cheap but not very accurate. Older babies may wriggle about too much to let you get a clear reading.

● Mercury thermometer: the old-fashioned type of glass thermometer needs to be held under the arm for a minute or two to give a clear reading (never put a mercury thermometer in your baby's mouth). The drawback with these thermometers is that they may be difficult to read and can get broken.

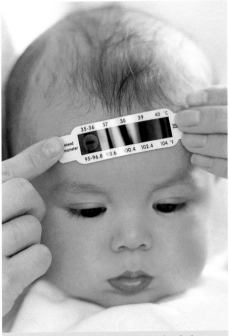

Temperature indicator strips are simple to use

● Ear thermometer: this type is placed just inside your baby's ear and gives an instant reading. They are quick and accurate, but by far the most expensive option.

What's normal? A temperature that's somewhere between 36°C and 37.5°C (96.8°F and 99.5°F), as shown on thermometers that are used in the mouth or the ear, is considered a normal body temperature. The body's external temperature is slightly lower, so if you take your baby's temperature using a thermometer on the forehead or under the arm, a normal reading would be somewhere between 35°C and 36.5°C

(95°F and 97.7°F). Body temperatures often increase in the afternoon and your baby's temperature may also be slightly higher if she has been crying for a while.

A high temperature If your baby has a temperature, try to cool her down by removing some of her clothes and making sure her head is uncovered. If she's over three months old, give her a dose of baby paracetamol and check her temperature again after an hour.

If her temperature remains high, remove all of her clothes and sponge tepid water over her head, body and limbs. Lie her on a towel to dry and put on the minimum of clothes (just a nappy).

If sponging does not work and her body temperature does not come down to 39°C (102.2°F) or lower within an hour, or if you have succeeded in cooling your baby down only for her temperature to rise again the next day, seek medical advice.

Keeping cool in bed It's always important that your baby doesn't become overheated at night and this is especially true when she is poorly. Her face may feel normal, but check how warm she really is by sliding your hand down inside her clothes so you can feel the skin on her back. If it feels hot, and particularly if she is sweating, take off a layer of bedding. Check her again half an hour later and remove more bedding if she is still too hot.

It is not advisable to give your baby any medicines (except baby paracetamol once she is over three months old) without consulting either your pharmacist or your doctor first.

Medicines by mouth Liquid medicines are measured in millilitres (mls) and it's best to measure out the dose before you pick your baby up. Hold your baby in your arms when you give her medicine and have a cloth handy to wipe up any spillages.
• Spoon – a standard teaspoon holds 5ml although very young babies may require a smaller dose. If necessary, your chemist can supply a plastic spoon for measuring out 2.5ml, for example.
• Syringe – draw up the medicine from the bottle. Squeeze a little back until you have the correct dose. Slip the syringe into the corner of your baby's mouth and press the plunger gently.
• Dropper – small amounts of liquid medicine may be given using a plastic (not glass) dropper.

Eye drops Lie your baby on her back and stand behind her head so she looks up at you. With your thumb, gently pull down on her cheek below the eye and squeeze the drops into the space between the eye and the lower lid. If she won't open her eyes, squeeze the drops into the hollow at the inner corner of her eye and gently roll the lower lid open to let the drops flow in.

Ear drops Lie your baby on her side with her poorly ear uppermost and let the drops fall into the ear opening. Move the ear lobe gently to help the drops sink in.

Suppositories These may be prescribed when a baby is vomiting and cannot take medicines by mouth. Moisten the suppository and slip it into her anus (back passage) with your little finger, inserting your finger as far as the end joint.

Giving medicines

First aid

Although you will do your very best to keep your baby safe, accidents do happen. Knowing how to treat her when she's hurt and recognising an emergency situation are vital skills

AT ITS SIMPLEST, first aid involves treating minor cuts and grazes. But if your baby is seriously hurt, then knowing how to carry out emergency first aid could make the difference between life and death.

Emergency ABC

If your baby has had an accident, or is sick and is unconscious, follow the emergency ABC procedure given below:
● A is for airway – make sure your baby's airway is not blocked.
● B is for breathing – if your baby isn't breathing, start artificial ventilation.
● C is for circulation – if your baby's heart isn't beating (which means blood is not circulating), start carrying out chest compressions with artificial ventilation.

If you are alone with your baby, you may need to carry out emergency first aid before you get help. If there is someone in the house with you, shout for help as you carry out first aid.

A is for airway To open the airway:
● Lay your baby on her back. Tilt her head back gently with one hand on her forehead

and a finger under her chin (see below). Lifting her chin will stop her tongue from falling back and blocking her throat which could impair her breathing.

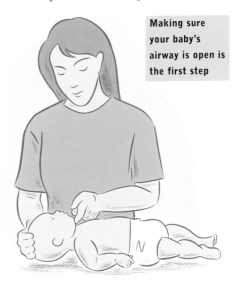

Making sure your baby's airway is open is the first step

● Check whether your baby is breathing for up to ten seconds. Put your ear close to her mouth and listen. Look to see if her chest is rising and falling.
● If your baby is not breathing, use artificial ventilation to breathe for her (see right). If she's breathing, hold her in your arms with her head down (see page 154). Dial 999.

B is for breathing To carry out artificial ventilation on your baby:

● Lay your baby on her back. Look in her mouth. Carefully remove anything obvious.

● Gently tilt your baby's head back by placing one hand on her forehead and one finger under her chin to lift her jaw (see left).

● Put your mouth over your baby's mouth and nose, and breathe gently into her lungs.

● Do this five times, then check her circulation by checking her pulse in the inside of the upper arm and assessing her colour.

● If there is no pulse, or the pulse detected is slow (at a rate of less than 60 beats per minute) start chest compressions with artificial ventilation (see right).

● If you can feel a pulse (and it's at more than 60 beats per minute), carry on breathing for your baby, using artificial ventilation for one minute, then call for an ambulance. Continue with artificial ventilation until your baby is breathing for herself.

If your baby has stopped breathing, you should use artificial ventilation to breathe for her

C is for circulation If your baby has no pulse, you should carry out chest compressions to try to pump blood around the body. You will need to combine this with artificial ventilation so that the blood is oxygenated.

● Lay your baby on her back. Place two fingertips on the lower breastbone. Press sharply down into her chest to a depth of about one third of her body.

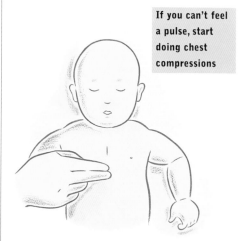

If you can't feel a pulse, start doing chest compressions

● Do this five times quite quickly – at a rate of about two compressions per second (or 100 compressions per minute) – then put your mouth over your baby's nose and mouth, and give her one breath as described in the artificial ventilation method (see left).

● Continue with five compressions to the chest, followed by one breath, for one minute. Call for an ambulance.

● Carry on with the chest compressions and artificial ventilation until help arrives.

The recovery position If your baby is unconscious, but is breathing and has a pulse, hold her in the 'recovery position' (see below) while you seek medical help. The recovery position helps keep her airway clear and prevents her from choking on her tongue or, if she's sick, on her vomit.

You can also use the recovery position if you've carried out the Emergency ABC procedure and your baby's heartbeat has returned and she is breathing for herself.

What to do
● To hold your baby in the recovery position, cradle her in both arms, holding her across your body, with her feet slightly higher than her head. Support her neck in the crook of your elbow.

The recovery position helps to keep the airway clear

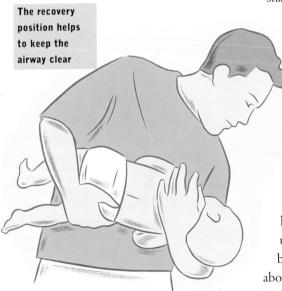

First aid for accidents

Prevention is the best way to protect your baby from harm (see page 125). But, if an accident does happen, first aid can give your baby the best chance of a safe recovery.

Choking Like adults, babies have a powerful reflex which allows them to cough up anything that threatens to block their windpipe. However, occasionally, when a baby is eating or is exploring something with her mouth, she will breathe in and inhale a piece of food or a small object which gets stuck in her windpipe.

What to do
● Hold your baby so that she is lying along your arm with her head down. Give her a sharp slap between the shoulder blades (see right). Repeat five times.

● If your baby is still choking, check inside her mouth and carefully remove any obvious obstruction with one finger.

● If she is still choking, lie her on her back and place two fingers in the centre of her chest on the lower breastbone. Press sharply downwards up to five times. If your baby is still choking, call for an ambulance. Continue with the above steps until medical help arrives. If she becomes unconscious, combine the above choking procedure with Emergency ABC procedures (see pages 152-153).

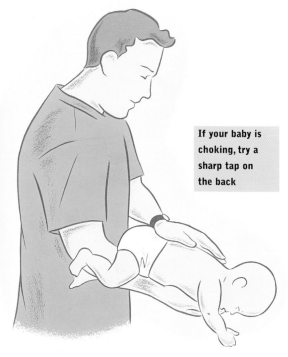

If your baby is choking, try a sharp tap on the back

Drowning It is quite possible for babies to drown in just a few centimetres of water – fishponds, baths, buckets with water in them and paddling pools are all dangerous, so never leave your baby unattended, especially when there's water nearby.

What to do

● Remove your baby from the water. Hold her in the recovery position (see left).

● If your baby is breathing, call for an ambulance. If she is very cold, you need to warm her up. Remove her wet clothes then hold her against your skin, inside your clothes. Wrap yourself in a blanket and walk around in a warm room until help arrives. Warm her up gradually – do not use a hot water bottle or put her close to a fire.

● If your baby is not breathing, start artificial ventilation (see page 153).

● If your baby's heart is not beating, begin chest compressions with artificial ventilation (see page 153).

Electric shock An electric shock can make your baby unconscious or can burn her. In severe cases, it can even result in death. If your baby has suffered a shock and is still in contact with the electrical current, don't touch her without taking precautions first (see below) – you could be electrocuted too.

What to do

● Switch off the electricity at the mains or at the plug. If you can't switch it off, stand on either a telephone directory, a thick pile of newspapers or a rubber mat and use a wooden pole, such as a broom handle or chair leg, to try and push your baby away from the electricity source.

● If your baby is not breathing, start to carry out artificial ventilation (see page 153).

● Check your baby's pulse. If she has no pulse, begin chest compressions with artificial ventilation (see page 153).

● If your baby is breathing, cool any burns with water and call for an ambulance.

Falls Even a very young baby can push herself off a changing mat or bed, so never leave her alone on either, even if you think she hasn't learnt to roll yet.

What to do

- If your baby is crying loudly and moving her arms and legs freely after a fall, she's probably all right. However, if in doubt, it's worth taking her to casualty for a check-up.
- If you think she may have damaged her neck or spine, do not move her unless absolutely necessary. Call an ambulance. If you need to move her to carry out emergency first aid, keep her head, body and legs aligned as you roll her over.
- If your baby loses consciousness, vomits or has clear or blood-stained discharge from her nose or ears, call an ambulance.

Poisoning Many accidents involving children are a result of swallowing cleaning fluids, medicines, cosmetics or poisonous plants. Poisoning can cause vomiting, unconsciousness and fits but, in some cases, these reactions may not occur for a while.

What to do

- Carry out Emergency ABC procedures, if necessary (see pages 152-153). Dial 999.
- Don't try to make your baby sick, but if she is, take the vomit to hospital, along with any fluid or plant you suspect may be involved. If her lips are burnt and she is conscious, rinse them with cold water or milk.

Scalds and burns If your baby suffers a burn or scald that causes rawness, swelling or blisters, or that covers a large part of her body, she'll need medical attention.

A cup of tea stays hot enough to scald your baby for 15 minutes. Every year more than 67,000 children have an accident in the kitchen – most are under four years old

What to do

- Cool the area by pouring cold water on it for at least ten minutes (20 minutes if the burn is caused by a chemical). Do not attempt to burst any blisters.
- Call for an ambulance as soon as possible.
- Carefully remove any clothing around the burn area, but do not try to loosen clothing that has stuck to the skin.
- Cover the burn with a wet, non-fluffy cotton cloth (such as a clean tea towel or pillow case) or a clean piece of cling-film. If the burn is on the face, leave uncovered and keep cooling it with water. Don't apply ointment, powder or grease.
- Wrap your baby in a warm blanket. Keep an eye on her – burns can cause shock, breathing difficulties and unconsciousness.

Learning first aid

The emergency procedures and accident advice given here is no substitute for attending a first aid training course. For details of courses being held in your area, contact your local branch of the British Red Cross or call their national headquarters for more information (see page 168).

Everyday **first aid**

Many minor accidents and day-to-day incidents do not require medical attention. These kind of accidents can be dealt with using basic first aid skills:

Minor burns If your baby has a very small, superficial burn, cool the area under cold, running water for ten minutes. Remove any clothes from around the burn then cover the area with a clean, non-fluffy cotton material. Be careful not to stick any plaster or sticky tape on the burnt area and do not use any kind of cream or ointment (see left). Large burns and burns that blister need medical attention – get your baby to hospital as soon as you can.

Stings Soothe insect stings by applying ice wrapped in a cotton cloth. If a bee has left its sting in, draw it out with tweezers first. Stings in the mouth can be dangerous as the swelling may obstruct breathing. If your baby is stung in the mouth, call for an ambulance or take her to hospital immediately.

Foreign bodies It's not unusual for babies to push small objects, such as beads or small pieces of food, into their nose or ear. If your baby has something in her nose or ear, do not attempt to remove it – take her to hospital. If she has an insect in her ear, lay her on her side and pour a cupful of warm water onto the ear – this may flush the insect out. If it's still stuck, seek medical help.

If your baby gets anything in her eye, stop her from rubbing it and try to wash it out as quickly as you can. Tilt her head back and pour clean water into the inner corner of the eye. If there is a foreign body embedded in the eye, or an object which is not easily removed, cover the eye and take your baby to hospital.

Cuts and grazes If the wound is dirty, wash it gently with water. Dry the wound and cover it with sterile gauze.

To stop bleeding from minor cuts, raise the injured part of the body until it is above the level of the heart and apply pressure to the cut. Once bleeding has stopped, apply a sticky plaster.

Minor bites If your baby has been bitten by an animal, wash the bite gently but thoroughly with soap and warm water. Gently dab the wound dry, then apply a clean dressing. Take your baby to see your doctor as she may also need a tetanus injection and antibiotics.

Your first aid kit To ensure that you are prepared for all minor accidents, equip your home with a basic first aid kit. Make sure that your partner or anyone who looks after your baby at home, such as a child minder or baby-sitter, knows where to find it. Your home first aid kit should contain the following items:
- Sticky plasters
- Blunt-ended scissors
- Tweezers
- Cotton wool
- Crepe bandage
- Gauze bandage
- Safety pins
- Surgical tape (Micropore™)
- Non-adhesive, sterile dressings
- Baby thermometer (with spare battery)
- Infant paracetamol with measuring spoon or dropper.

A-Z of baby health

Asthma

Asthma is an inflammatory disease of the airways of the lungs which results in coughing, wheezing and shortness of breath. It often runs in families and is more common in children who suffer from eczema and hayfever. Asthma is a growing problem – twice as many children develop it now as they did in the 1970s, with around one in ten children needing some form of asthma treatment by the time they go to school.

Symptoms Coughing and wheezing are usually the first signs in a young baby. Both tend to be worse in the early hours of the morning and often follow a cold. Children normally develop asthma before the age of five but most grow out of it by their late teens. However, around a third will need to take medication for the rest of their life.

What to do There is some evidence that breast-feeding and delaying weaning until at least four months may reduce the chances of your baby developing asthma. This may be more important if there is a strong family history of the condition.

Don't smoke – babies living in a house where parents smoke are more likely to suffer with chest problems. Most asthmatics have an allergy of some sort, most commonly to house dust mites and pets. Keep all pets and animals off soft furnishings and out of your baby's room and take steps to reduce house dust mites. Contact the National Asthma Campaign for advice (see page 169).

In most children, asthma is fairly easy to control, using a combination of drugs. These are best given in some form of inhaler and even young children can manage these with a bit of patience. Unfortunately, the drugs are not always that effective in young babies under the age of 12 months but asthma is often not as serious in this age group.

Chickenpox

Chickenpox is a common childhood viral infection and is one of the most infectious diseases in the world. It's spread through coughing and sneezing, and although the same virus causes shingles, adults cannot catch shingles from children with chickenpox.

Symptoms High temperature is typically the first sign, with the characteristic rash appearing some two days later. Symptoms appear ten to 21 days after contact with someone with chickenpox and a child is contagious until all of the sores have scabbed over.

What to do Keep your baby cool to reduce the extent of the rash. Cut her nails to minimise scratching. Calamine lotion may help relieve some of the itch, but crops of blisters

in and around the mouth, genitals or anus may need treatment from your doctor.

Avoid contact with pregnant women. For the one in 20 pregnant women who are not immune to chickenpox, infection within the first 20 weeks of pregnancy can be risky for both the mother and her unborn baby.

Conjunctivitis

See Eye problems.

Convulsions

See Febrile convulsions.

Cot death

See page 103.

Coughs and colds

There are over 200 different types of virus that cause coughs and colds. Young babies are particularly susceptible to them and it's perfectly normal for babies to get as many as ten coughs and colds in their first year. Most colds disappear as quickly as they come and rarely cause any serious problems.

What to do Seek medical advice if you're worried that your baby may have more than a simple cough or cold, or if:

● your baby is prone to asthma

● she's having difficulty feeding (young babies have to breathe through their nose when they are feeding – colds make this very difficult)

● she is making funny noises when she breathes (see Asthma and Croup)

● she is breathing faster than normal.

Avoid cough medicines – they won't help most children and should not be given to young babies. Proprietary cold remedies should not be given to babies either, although nose drops and infant paracetamol may be helpful – ask your health visitor, GP or pharmacist for advice if your baby is under three months old.

Cradle cap

See Eczema.

Croup

Croup is a viral infection of the main airways leading into the lungs. It's a common condition that tends to occur in epidemics during the autumn and the spring.

Symptoms Croup starts with what appears to be a normal cough or cold, but after a few days the child loses her voice and develops a barking, dry cough. The most worrying aspect of croup is that it makes breathing in difficult – the voice box becomes swollen and the child sounds hoarse when she breathes in. In babies, breathing tends to become more difficult when they are excited or upset, and they seem particularly prone to problems during the early hours of the morning.

What to do Most cases of croup settle without special treatment. Humidifying the air in your baby's room by leaving a kettle boiling for two or three minutes may help, but never leave the kettle unattended.

If your baby is having problems breathing and is distressed, try to comfort her. This is often all that is required but if it fails to ease her breathing, seek medical advice. A small number of cases are best admitted to hospital for observation. Worrying signs include sudden onset of symptoms, high fever (temperature over 39°C/102.2°F), drooling, colour changes (looking pale or blue) and rapid breathing (more than 60 breaths per minute). All these symptoms require urgent medical assessment.

Diarrhoea

Diarrhoea can be caused by a number of conditions but, in most cases, they get better of their own accord and are nothing to worry about. For a young baby with diarrhoea the main danger is the possibility of dehydration – babies become dehydrated far more quickly than adults. Dehydration is more likely to occur if the diarrhoea is accompanied by vomiting (see page 167).

The symptoms of dehydration can come on gradually and may not all be present at the same time. Tiny, newborn babies are more at risk than healthy, older ones. Look out for the following signs if you suspect that your baby may be dehydrated:
- Your baby's mouth and lips are dry
- Her nappies are dry or less wet than usual and her urine is a darker colour
- Your baby is listless and not interested in anything
- She is more sleepy than usual
- The fontanelle (the soft spot on top of your baby's head) appears to be sunken
- Her eyes look sunken
- Your baby is weak and floppy
- Her skin is dry, pale or mottled.

What to do Seek medical advice if diarrhoea persists for more than 24 hours or your baby's stools contain blood. Also seek advice if diarrhoea is accompanied by vomiting or if your baby appears to be in any discomfort. Make sure you give your baby plenty of fluids. Buy rehydration mixtures from your pharmacist or make your own by adding eight teaspoons of sugar and half a teaspoon of salt to one litre (2¼ pints) of boiled water. (For babies under six months, omit the salt.) Ask your pharmacist how much to give. If your baby can't keep fluids down and appears dehydrated (see box, left), call your doctor. Never give anti-diarrhoeal medications to young children. Feed your baby as you would normally, unless your doctor directs otherwise. There is no evidence that diluting milk makes any difference to most cases of diarrhoea.

Ear problems

Hearing difficulties A newborn baby can hear and will react to a sudden sound with a startled movement. Within a few weeks, she'll respond to quieter sounds and to her mother's voice, although she may not turn to see where sounds come from for a few months. When your baby is around eight months, her hearing will be tested by your health visitor. But, if you feel your baby isn't hearing properly, consult your GP who may refer you to a specialist. Because you are with your baby all the time, you are in the best position to judge whether she can hear properly.

Middle ear infections The middle ear is deep in the head, behind the ear drum and very close to the back of the throat, especially in a baby where everything is tiny. Normally the middle ear contains air, but when a baby has a cold, the middle ear may fill with fluid which can become infected and painful. Living in a home where there are smokers means a baby is more likely to get middle ear infections.

Symptoms Your baby may have no obvious symptoms – she may simply be miserable, full of cold and feverish. Sometimes, if her ear is painful, she will pull at it (although she may also do this for fun because she's just discovered it). Occasionally, the ear will look red or there may be a discharge from the ear.

What to do If you suspect an ear infection, seek medical advice. Most ear infections are caused by a virus and will get better on their own, but some require antibiotics. If your baby is over three months old, you can give her baby paracetamol for the pain and wipe away any discharge. Never probe the ear with a cotton bud or anything else.

Eczema

Around one in ten children develops eczema and there are a number of different types. Atopic eczema causes dry, red patches, particularly on the inside of elbows and the backs of knees. It's associated with hayfever and asthma, and often runs in families. Most children grow out of atopic eczema by their early teens but it can be severe in some cases. The second most common type is seborrhoeic eczema which usually causes a scaly rash behind the ears and on the scalp (also known as cradle cap).

What to do Breast-feeding and delaying weaning until at least four months may help make eczema less likely, particularly if there is a strong family history of the condition.

The key to successful eczema control is good skin care. Avoid unnecessary soaps and bubble baths – if you do use them, ask your pharmacist for skin-friendly types and keep your baby's skin well moisturised.

Although dietary factors undoubtedly play a role in some babies with eczema, it can be an exasperating task trying to find the trigger. Seek your doctor's advice before eliminating foods from your baby's diet.

Always use prescribed medicines as directed – steroid creams work well for all types of eczema and are safe if used properly. They should only be used where eczema is causing distress and are not a substitute for good basic skin care.

Keep your baby's nails short and try to dress her in cool, natural fibres. Keep exposure to house dust mites and pets to a minimum.

For more advice and information, contact the National Eczema Society (see page 169).

Eye problems

Blocked tear duct The eyes produce tears all the time, not just when we cry. Normally, tears drain down a tiny tube from the inner corner of the eye into the nose, but sometimes this tube is not fully developed in babies. As a result, tears spill out onto the cheek and may cause repeated bouts of conjunctivitis (see below). By the time your baby is a year old, the tear duct will almost certainly have opened, although occasionally surgery is needed to clear the duct.

Conjunctivitis Also known as sticky eye, conjunctivitis is common in babies and young children. Sometimes it is caused by a blocked tear duct (see above); other times by a virus or bacteria. Sometimes conjunctivitis in a baby less than two weeks old is caused by an organism called chlamydia, which is acquired from the birth canal.

Symptoms The white of the eye may look pink. A yellowish discharge collects in the inner corner of the eye and along the eyelashes and may even stick the eyelids together.

What to do Gently wipe the eyes using cotton wool dipped in warm, boiled water, using a fresh piece for each wipe. If there is still discharge after 24 hours, see your doctor as your baby may need antibiotic drops. Conjunctivitis is very infectious, so prevent it spreading through the family by making sure everyone has their own towel and flannel.

Squint A squint, where one of the eyes wanders, is not uncommon in newborn babies. By the time a baby is three months old, her eyes should be straight and working together. Some babies have a wide fold of skin between the nose and the eye, and this may give the appearance of a squint when they look sideways. If you think your baby has a squint, consult your health visitor or GP. The sooner a squint is treated, the better the eyes respond.

Febrile convulsions

This is a seizure associated with a high temperature in children under the age of five, with no obvious cause. One in 30 children has at least one febrile convulsion. They are not a sign of future epilepsy, although three in every 100 children who have convulsions will go on to develop it. The key to dealing with febrile convulsions is to prevent them by keeping feverish children cool. For information on how to reduce a baby's temperature, see page 151.

Symptoms Similar to epileptic seizures, febrile convulsions are characterised by involuntary muscular contractions which make the body twitch and jerk. They usually last just a few minutes, but in rare cases, up to 20 minutes.

What to do If your baby has a seizure, do not try to restrain her. Lay her on her side somewhere safe and ensure her mouth and airway are clear. Call for medical help as soon as the seizure has finished – they rarely last more than a few minutes. Children who have experienced their first seizure are often admitted to hospital for investigation.

Fever

See pages 150-151.

Fits

See Febrile convulsions.

Genital problems in boys

Inflamed foreskin Also known as balanitis, this occurs when the foreskin becomes infected, usually as a result of being inside a nappy 24 hours a day.

Symptoms The end of your son's penis will become red, swollen and sore. There may even be a pus-like discharge.

What to do See your GP who may prescribe antibiotics. Do not try to pull your baby's foreskin back; it won't retract until he is three or four years old. However, do wash the penis thoroughly without soap at least once a day, especially when changing a dirty nappy.

Tight foreskin Occasionally the opening of a baby boy's foreskin is too tight, causing the skin to fill with urine and balloon out whenever he passes water. If you notice this happening, see your doctor who'll be able to tell you whether circumcision is necessary. Left untreated, a tight foreskin can lead to balanitis (see above) and urine infections.

Undescended testes Usually both testicles will have descended into the scrotum by the time a baby boy is born. However, in one in 50 boys they remain stuck inside the groin or the abdomen.

Symptoms You should be able to feel two soft, marble-sized lumps in your son's scrotum – these are his testicles. The best time to feel for them is when he is warm and relaxed, in his bath for example.

What to do Don't worry if you can't locate the testes – some boys have a sensitive reflex that pulls the testicles high into the scrotum. Your GP should routinely examine your baby's testicles anyway. Undescended testicles are best operated on at around 12 months.

Hernia

A hernia occurs when an organ or tissue bulges through a weakness in its muscular covering. The most common types in babies are in the groin (inguinal) and in and around the tummy button (umbilical). Not all need treatment but, left to their own devices, some become twisted or stuck which requires urgent surgery.

What to do Seek medical advice if you notice an abnormal lump in your baby's groin or abdomen. Groin hernias are best repaired surgically. Umbilical hernias rarely require treatment and are so common that they can almost be regarded as normal. Most umbilical hernias disappear within six months, although some children may have them up to school age.

Hip problems

Around one in 100 newborn babies has slightly unstable hips requiring observation over the first few months. Every baby's hips should be checked in the first few days of life and again at six weeks. Hip problems are more common in babies with a strong family history of the condition and those who are born in the breech position. Babies with unstable hips should be referred to an orthopaedic surgeon although most just need careful monitoring.

Immunisation

In her first year, your baby will be offered protection against a number of serious diseases. These include:

● Diphtheria – a severe throat and chest illness, often fatal. Now rare in the UK but present in some other countries.

● Tetanus – causes severe muscle spasms and can be fatal. There are around 20 cases a year in the UK, caught from contaminated soil.

● Whooping cough – can be severe, especially in tiny babies. May lead to lung damage.

● Polio – a paralysing disease. Can be fatal.

● HiB – an ear, throat and chest infection which, until widespread immunisation, was a common cause of bacterial meningitis.

The schedule for immunisation in the first year is as follows:

At two months	Polio	By mouth
	HiB Diphtheria Tetanus Whooping cough	One injection
At three months	Polio	By mouth
	HiB Diphtheria Tetanus Whooping cough	One injection
At four months	Polio	By mouth
	HiB Diphtheria Tetanus Whooping cough	One injection

In addition, an immunisation programme using the new meningitis C vaccine is underway. Protection is also available against:

● TB – if your baby is likely to be exposed to TB or has relatives with the disease, she will be offered the BCG immunisation.

● MMR – At 12 to 15 months, your child will be offered immunisation against measles, mumps and rubella (MMR).

Your baby needs to be well whenever she goes for immunisation.

Measles

Measles is now rare thanks to immunisation. It is spread by coughing and sneezing, and has an incubation period of seven to 21 days. Children are infectious for up to five days after the rash develops.

Symptoms Initially children experience cold-like symptoms with a fever, followed by a red rash which typically starts behind the ears and spreads down the whole body. Children with measles often develop conjunctivitis.

What to do Most children make a complete recovery and need no special treatment, but it is important to control fevers (see page 151). In rare cases measles can be very serious and can damage unborn babies. If your baby has measles, she should be kept away from other people and especially pregnant women.

Meningitis

An inflammation of the membranes which cover the brain, meningitis occurs in babies much less frequently than it used to. This is because the HiB jab gives protection against the haemophilus germ which used to be one of the most common causes.

Meningococcal meningitis (which exists in two forms, Group B and Group C) is the most serious form of meningitis. It can cause long-term disability and, in some cases, is fatal. Immediate treatment with antibiotics is absolutely vital and full recovery is possible if the right treatment is given in time.

Symptoms For a full list of symptoms for meningitis, see page 148.

What to do Meningitis requires emergency treatment. If you suspect that your baby has meningitis, seek medical advice immediately.

Mumps

A viral infection spread by coughing and sneezing, mumps is now rare thanks to immunisation. It has an incubation period of two to three weeks and children are contagious from seven days before and up to nine days after symptoms develop.

Symptoms Typically, a high temperature and a feeling of being unwell, plus painful swelling of the salivary glands in front of the ears, which gives the classic mumps appearance. In older boys and young men, mumps can cause inflammation of the testicles and, rarely, infertility. Mumps is also recognised as a cause of meningitis.

What to do Mumps requires no special treatment but fevers should be kept under control (for more information on how to bring down a baby's temperature, see page 151).

Rashes

Impetigo A bacterial infection of the skin causing red, weepy spots, usually around the nose and mouth.

What to do See your GP who will prescribe antibiotics. Impetigo is highly infectious so look out for signs in other family members.

Milk rash Tiny white spots around the mouth and on the face of very young babies.

What to do No special treatment is required and the rash will disappear of its own accord.

Nappy rash Occurs when the sensitive skin on a baby's bottom is damaged by wet and dirty nappies, or becomes infected with the yeast candida albicans (thrush).

Symptoms The skin becomes sore, red and sometimes spotty. In the case of nappy rash, spots and soreness tend not to occur in the folds of the skin. However, if the folds are affected, thrush may have developed. Nappy rash is often more common during teething.

What to do The best way to prevent nappy rash is by changing your baby's nappy frequently and using a barrier cream to protect her skin. If your baby has nappy rash, start changing her nappy more often, making sure her bottom is completely clean and dry before you put on a new nappy.

If possible, let your baby kick on her changing mat without a nappy for a while – this will allow the fresh air to get to the skin. If the nappy rash persists, your baby may have developed thrush. In this case, take her to see your doctor, who will be able to prescribe an appropriate cream.

Petechial rash A flat, dark red or purplish rash of bloodspots which can be a symptom of meningitis (see page 148) as well as of other less serious illnesses. Unlike other rashes, a petechial rash does not fade when a glass tumbler is pressed against it.
What to do If you suspect your baby has a petechial rash, seek immediate medical advice, even if your baby has no other symptoms.

Viral rashes A rash that starts on your baby's face or chest and then spreads to the rest of her body is generally caused by a virus.
What to do Often viral illnesses require no special treatment and your baby will get better once the illness has run its course. However, it is advisable to contact your doctor.

Slapped cheek syndrome Also known as fifth disease, this is a mild viral infection that's common in young children.
Symptoms Red, flat blotches with raised areas appear on the face.
What to do No specific treatment is required except to reduce high fevers (see page 151), and avoid contact with pregnant women.

Rubella

Better known as german measles, this condition has become less common thanks to the introduction of the MMR vaccine. All babies are now offered a vaccine at around 12 months and then again before they go to school. Rubella has an incubation period of 14 to 21 days and children are infectious from five days before until five days after the rash develops.
Symptoms A mild disease which causes little more than a rash, swollen glands at the back of the neck and a mild fever in most children. However, if german measles is caught by a pregnant woman, it can seriously damage the unborn baby. The first 12 weeks of pregnancy is the most dangerous period.
What to do Rubella requires no specific treatment and most children make a full recovery within a week or so. However, because rubella can damage unborn babies, anyone with the disease who comes into contact with a pregnant woman should make sure she is told so that she can seek advice from her doctor.

Teething

Some babies teeth as early as four months, many around the six-month mark and a few not until they are a year old. Heredity tends to determine the teething schedule, so if you or your partner teethed unusually early or late, your baby may do the same.

The first teeth to appear are normally the two centre teeth in the lower jaw, followed by the two centre teeth in the upper jaw. Four more teeth then emerge at the front before your baby cuts her first four back teeth. There are 20 milk teeth in all and most will appear by the time your child is two and a half and will last until she's about seven years old.

Symptoms and what to do

● Drooling – in some babies, teething may stimulate the production of saliva. This can make the area around the mouth sore and a rash sometimes develops. To avoid soreness, wipe your baby's mouth gently and often, and use a barrier cream to protect her skin.

● Chewing – teething babies often gnaw at anything within reach to try to relieve the pain of new teeth pushing their way through the gum. Try offering your baby a piece of carrot or a chilled teething ring to bite on.

● Changes in behaviour – your baby may be bad-tempered and waking more often than usual when she's teething. If she appears to be suffering, teething gels help by numbing gums.

● Loose bowels – your baby's stools may be looser than normal due to teething. However, teething doesn't cause diarrhoea, a high temperature or floppiness. If any of these symptoms occur, talk to your GP.

Taking care of your baby's milk teeth is important – they need to last her at least five years. To keep them healthy:
● **Give** your baby a balanced diet (for more details, see page 116)
● **Don't** let your baby go to sleep on a bottle of juice or milk
● **Make** water her main drink between meals. If she has fruit juice, dilute it well
● **Buy** a baby toothbrush and toothpaste, and make daily brushing part of her routine as soon as a few teeth appear
● **Start** dental check-ups early. Dental care is free for children, so register as soon as your baby has several teeth.

Urinary infections

Urinary infections are not common in babies, but should be taken seriously. If they are not properly investigated and treated, they can lead to kidney problems later in life.

Symptoms Your baby's urine should normally be clear and very pale yellow. If her urinary system is infected, nappies may be stained with dark or even pink urine which smells fishy or different to usual. She will probably also be unwell, feverish and off her feeds.

What to do Your doctor may wish to test your baby's urine and will probably give you a plastic bag specially designed for catching urine samples. If your baby does have an infection, she will be prescribed antibiotics and may be referred to a specialist who will check that your baby's bladder and kidneys are working properly.

Vomiting

Lots of babies bring up a little milk after a feed; this is classed as normal and is not vomiting. Real vomiting – when a lot of feed comes up – is sometimes the symptom of a relatively minor problem, such as a stomach virus, a reaction to a new food or overfeeding. However, occasionally it is the sign of something more serious, such as poisoning or meningitis (see page 148), especially when accompanied by other symptoms. In addition, prolonged vomiting can cause dehydration (see page 160).

What to do If your child vomits more than twice in 24 hours contact your GP or health visitor for advice.

Useful contacts

Action on Pre-Eclampsia, 31–33 College Rd, Harrow, HA1 1EJ. 020 8427 4217

Active Birth Centre, 113a Chetwynd Rd, London NW5 1DA. 020 7482 5554

Antenatal Results and Choices, 73 Charlotte St, London W1P 1LB. 020 7631 0285. Information about antenatal testing and support for those who have had a termination due to abnormalities

Association for Postnatal Illness, 25 Jerdan Place, London SW6 1BE. 020 7386 0868

Birth Defects Foundation, Martindale, Hawks Green, Cannock, Staffs, WS11 2XN. 08700 707020

BLISS, 2nd Floor, 89 Albert Embankment, London SE1 7TP. 020 7820 9471. Support for parents of babies in intensive care

British Acupuncture Council, 63 Jeddo Rd, London W12 9HQ. 020 8735 0400

British Chiropractic Association, Blagrave House, 17 Blagrave St, Reading, RG1 1QB. 0118 950 5950

British Diabetic Association, 10 Queen Anne St, London W1M 0BD. 020 7323 1531

British Homeopathic Association, 27a Devonshire St, London W1N 1RJ. 020 7935 2163

British Red Cross, 9 Grosvenor Crescent, London SW1X 7EJ. 020 7235 5454

Child Accident Prevention Trust, 4th Floor, Clerks Court, 18–20 Farringdon Lane, London, EC1R 3HA. 020 7608 3828

Cleft Lip and Palate Association (CLAPA), 235-237 Finchley Road, London NW3 6LS. 020 7431 0033

Contact a Family, 170 Tottenham Court Rd, London W1P 0HA. 020 7383 3555. Support for the parents of children with special needs

Daycare Trust, Shoreditch Town Hall Annexe, 380 Old St, London EC1V 9LT. 020 7739 2866

Down's Syndrome Association, 155 Mitcham Rd, London SW17 9PG. 020 8682 4001

Drinkline, 0800 917 8282. For drinkers who want help cutting back or giving up

Foundation for the Study of Infant Deaths, 14 Halkin St, London SW1X 7DP. 020 7235 1721

Gingerbread, 16–17 Clerkenwell Close, London EC2R 0AA. 020 7336 8183. Support for single parents

Home-Start, 2 Salisbury Rd, Leicester, LE1 7QR. 0116 233 9955

Independent Midwives Association, 1 The Great Quarry, Guildford, Surrey GU1 3XN. 01483 821104

La Leche League, BM Box 3424, London WC1N 3XX. 020 7242 1278. Support and advice on breast-feeding

Maternity Alliance, 45 Beech St, London EC2P 2LX. 020 7588 8582. Information on legal rights during pregnancy and after birth

Meet-a-Mum Association (MAMA), 26 Avenue Rd, South Norwood, London SE25 4DX. 020 8771 5595. Support group for those suffering from postnatal depression

MENCAP, 123 Golden Lane, London EC1Y ORT. 020 7696 5593/5503. Support for parents of children with learning disabilities

Miscarriage Association, Clayton Hospital, Northgate, Wakefield, WF1 3JS. 01924 200799

National Asthma Campaign, Providence House, Providence Place, London N1 0NP. 020 7226 2260

National Childbirth Trust, Alexandra House, Oldham Terrace, London W3 6NH. 020 8992 8637

National Childminding Association, 8 Masons Hill, Bromley, Kent BR2 9EY. 020 8464 6164

National Eczema Society, 163 Eversholt Street, London NW1 1BU. 020 7388 4097

National Institute of Medical Herbalists, 56 Longbrook St, Exeter, EX4 6AH. 01392 426022

National Meningitis Trust, Fern House, Bath Rd, Stroud, Glos GL5 3TJ. 0345 538118

Osteopathic Information Service, 176 Tower Bridge Rd, London SE1 3LU. 020 7357 6655

Parents at Work, 5th Floor, 45 Beech St, London EC2Y 8AD. 020 7628 3565

Positively Women, 347–349 City Rd, London EC1V 1LR. 020 7713 0222. Support for women with HIV and Aids and their families

Quitline, 0800 002200. Help for smokers who want to give up

Relate, 01788 573241 for your nearest branch

Royal Society for the Prevention of Accidents, Edgbaston Park, 353 Bristol Rd, Birmingham, B5 7ST. 0121 248 2000

SCOPE, 6 Market Rd, London N7 9PW. 020 7619 7100. Help for parents and children with cerebral palsy

Serene, BM Crysis, London WC1N 3XX. 020 7404 5011. Support for the mothers of babies who cry all the time

Sickle Cell Society, 54 Station Rd, London NW10 4UA. 020 8961 7795

Society of Homeopaths, 2 Artizan Rd, Northampton, NN1 4HU. 01604 621400

Still Birth and Neonatal Death Society (SANDS), 28 Portland Place, London W1N 4DE. 020 7436 5881

The Pregnancy Shop, 0870 166 8899 Specialist pregnancy products by post

The Real Nappy Association, PO Box 374, London SE26 4RX. 020 8299 4519

The Vegetarian Society, Parkdale, Dunham Rd, Altrincham, Cheshire WA14 4QG. 0161 925 2000

Toxoplasmosis Trust, 61–71 Collier St, London N1 9BE. 020 7713 0599

Twins and Multiple Birth Association (TAMBA), Harnott House, 309 Chester Rd, Little Sutton, Ellesmere Port CH66 1QQ. 0151 348 0020

Index

Acknowledgments

Photographs Amy Neunsinger, Anthony Blake, Ashley Stephenson, Bubbles, Daniel Paingbourne, Image Bank, Images Colour Library, Jens Storch, Julian Cotton, Kim Golding, Lennart Nilsson, Moose Azim, Mother & Baby, Reed Davis, Retna, Robert Harding, Science Photo Library, Simon Archer, Sunday Mirror, MSI, Superstock, Telegraph Colour Library, Tesco, Tom Main, Tony Stone, Trevor Vaughan
Cover photograph Kim Golding **Illustrations** Jane Spencer
Thanks to Active Birth Centre, Earthlings Clothing (California), Harry Duley, Pineapple
First Aid The information on pp152-157 was validated by the British Red Cross on 20/9/99.